THE GOLDEN DAWN LEGACY VOLUME I

A Solomonic Magical Circle, (c. 1572)

The Golden Dawn Legacy

VOLUME I.

THE MAGICAL WRITINGS

OF

FLORENCE FARR.

EDITED AND Foreword BY
DARCY KÜNTZ.

INTRODUCTION by
CAROLINE WISE.

2012
GOLDEN DAWN RESEARCH TRUST

THE GOLDEN DAWN LEGACY VOLUME I:
THE MAGICAL WRITINGS OF FLORENCE FARR

••○○○ ○ ○•••

ISBN: 978-1-926982-02-1.

Revised and Corrected Edition.
First Printing, 2012.

GOLDEN DAWN RESEARCH TRUST
P.O. Box 15964 Austin, Texas 78761-5964 USA

Contents

Illustrations

Foreword

Florence Beatrice Farr was born on 7 July 1860 in Bromley, Kent. In 1873, at the age of thirteen, she was sent to Cheltenham Ladies' College in Gloucestershire. In 1877 she entered Queen's College in London which was the first college to admit women and by 1880 she left the College. In 1881 she began her acting career with the study of Shakespeare and "step-dancing" under J.L. Toole in his small theatre at Charing Cross. On 14 August 1883 her father, William Farr, died. In 1884 she met the actor Edward Emery and on 31 December she married him. In 1888 Florence separated from her husband who moved to America and on 4 February 1895 her divorce was finalized.

In July 1890 Florence was initiated into the Neophyte Grade of the Isis-Urania Temple of the Golden Dawn. She took the motto Sapientia Sapienti Dono Data (Wisdom is given to the wise as a gift). On 2 August 1891 Florence entered the Portal Grade and on 22 December 1891 she was initiated into the Adeptus Minor Grade.

For the first half of 1892 Florence Farr was the Cancellarius of the Isis-Urania Temple. In March 1893 she took the office of the Praemonstrator after Westcott resigned. She remained in the office until she was appointed the Chief Adept in Anglia on 1 April 1897. The schism of 1900 was the beginning of the end for the Golden Dawn which saw the expulsion of S.L. Mathers from the Order. Florence resigned completely from the Golden Dawn in the fall of 1902.

She continued her writing until she moved to Jaffna, Ceylon and become the principal of the Ramanathan Hindu

Girls' College on 5 September 1912. There she died of breast Cancer on 29 April 1917.

The history of Florence Farr and other women of the Golden Dawn can be read in Mary K. Greer's excellent book, *Women of the Golden Dawn: Rebels and Priestesses*. Rochester, VT: Park Street Press, 1995.

Florence Farr was a strong woman who was involved in areas that were generally dominated by men. She helped bring Irish drama to life and added the magic to many Golden Dawn rituals. Her literary and magical contributions have not been fully appreciated. In her time she had written a number of books and articles on magic and drama as well as a number of important Golden Dawn Grade papers—not to mention the quality of her Golden Dawn diaries and note-books. This collection of articles and books will show a depth of understanding and wisdom of the Golden Dawn system that is unrivalled by any author of the Golden Dawn today.

It is hoped that this collection of Magical exploration by Florence Farr is well received in the spirit it was written.

DARCY KÜNTZ,
Austin, Texas,
Revised 2012.

Introduction
Florence Farr, Priestess and Adept

"We are priestesses of that pure flame, whose temple is the soul" spoken by Amaryllis, Priestess of Selene in *A Sicilian Idyll* by John Todhunter.

"Come to me. Come to me, for my speech hath in it the power to protect, and it possesseth life. I am Isis the goddess, and I am the lady of words of power." Spoken by Isis from *The Egyptian Book of the Dead* translated by Sir E.A. Wallis Budge.

BICKLEY in Kent in the 1860s conjures up images of dull and gentile suburbia. Zooming in closer, it becomes far more interesting, being a stone's throw from those mysterious caverns the Chislehurst Caves. It is also near to the enigmatic Kent 'Crays' and to Scadbury Park, with its 'Dragon Men' intrigues. It was at Bickley that Florence Beatrice Farr was born on the 7th of July 1860. She was named after Florence Nightingale, a colleague of her father's.

Cheltenham Ladies College mentions Florence Farr as a "notable former pupil". She later attended Queens College, the first college of higher education of girls in London. Despite her good and progressive education, in the 1910 publication *In Modern Women, Her Intentions*, Florence had this to say:

"... six years to get out of the shell my education [had] hardened around me. I don't suppose I should ever have spread my own wings if the beak of my destiny had not been stronger than my overwhelming education, so that it succeeded in hammering through that shell at last."

Breaking this shell, Farr had tried her hand at teaching, and then became an actress. She also tried directing, she composed, she was a novelist, a playwright, a journalist, an advocate of women's equality, and a musician. All of these threads combined in making her a superb magician and priestess.

She mixed with the artistic Bohemian set around Bedford Park in West London; playwrights, poets, socialists and intellectuals. She counted the family of William Morris as her friends. It was among this circle that she met the poet W. B. Yeats who became a lifelong friend and collaborator.

Florence was initiated into the Isis-Urania Temple of the Hermetic Order of the Golden Dawn in July 1890, around the time of her 30th birthday. Yeats had introduced her to the Mathers' at the home of Helena Blavatsky. Yeats had seen the magical potential in his friend Farr when she appeared as a priestess in John Todhunter's romantic play *A Sicilian Idyll*. In the play, which was probably inspired by Farr, she played Amaryllis, a Priestess of the moon goddess Selene. She inhabited the part of the priestess well, her grace captivating Yeats.

The words from *The Egyptian Book of the Dead* attributed to Isis and quoted at the beginning of this piece lend themselves well to Florence Farr. She had many associations with the Egyptian Goddess Isis, the mistress of Magic, and also with the Book of the Dead of which she had made of a study, the translation by Budge being completed in 1895. Florence understood better than most members of the Golden Dawn the magic of speech. She knew the importance of the magical voice. The correct intonation in ritual and evocation, with patterns of speech and tone, brought about changes in consciousness and aided contact with the divine. She was interested in exploring the use of sound and music, and its correct application in magical and artistic endeavours. She saw the importance of rhythm, of chant, and of incantation.

Yeats said of her recitals: "Speech was music, the poetry acquired a nobility, a passionate austerity that made it akin for certain moments to the great poetry of the world."

Farr's Hermetic study was broad, as Darcy Küntz shows here, but she was no dilettante. She was not an 'air-head' as I have seen her described: her mystical interests were far-removed from those of a self-centered naval gazer. As well as her studies and writings, she was immersed in the running of the Order, in ceremonial work, in experimental work, and in teaching and training initiates and students.

Some of Farr's evocations and scrying work were looked on with suspicion, being seen as daring and even dangerous. They brought about the ire of Annie Horniman for one. Certainly they were bold and innovative; but Farr the magician was not one for 'incorrect practice', and had confidence in her knowledge and skills that she had invested so much time in honing. Precision was her by-word in magic.

She wrote on Rosicrucianism, of symbols, of Kabbalah, Alchemy, Enochian, Vedanta, and philosophy. Along with her astral experiments, all were driven by her belief that adepthood was perfection of the mind and body. Control of the will led to becoming one with the divine. She said that:

> "Only the merging of our human wills with the Universal Will can result in hastening the day of our perfection. If we labour against the world's will we shall fail and our work will vanish from of the face of the earth."

The Golden Dawn and its ceremonial rituals and correspondences rooted in the Kabbalistic Tree of Life would be the vehicle for this attainment. Her experimental theatrical and recital work "in the outer" complimented this.

The Egyptian arcana were especially important for the Golden Dawn and for Farr. She immersed herself in Egyptian studies at the British Museum, and of Ancient Egyptian cosmology she said, "The first necessity of the study of magic among the Egyptians was cultivated of all the faculties dormant in human nature." Of the Egyptian adepts she said that they "gained power by the identification of themselves with the types of natural forces, known to us as gods."

To Farr, "The most potent magical formula was the identification of the Ritualist with the God whose power he was invoking."

This magical philosophy is reflected in her play *The Shrine of the Golden Hawk*. In 1902, Farr had resigned from the Golden Dawn and had joined the Theosophical Society. In her play, written around this time, her protagonist Nectoris, who is "skilled in the mysteries of Isis", declares:

> "I look unharmed upon the face of the god because his eyes are my eyes, and his power is my power, his spirit is my spirit. I am an Egyptian and mistress of the mysteries. I have become one with Heru, for I have eaten of his substance and I have drunk of his spirit, and I am henceforth ruler of the holy places. Whoso is made one with the gods makes their holy places desolate, and himself becomes their sanctuary; and his being is greater than theirs, being made of their own substance. For he has devoured their mystical rites and symbols, he has swallowed their shining forms, he has eaten the power and wisdom of every god, and the period of his life is eternity!"

In *Egyptian Magic* she writes:

> "To the Ancient Egyptians the most eminent man was he who had by hard training gained supremacy over the Elements, from which his own body and the Manifested World were alike formed; one whose Will had risen Phoenix-like from the ashes of his desires; one whose intuition cleansed from the stains

of material illusion, was a clear mirror in which he could perceive the Past, the Present and the Future."

The mystical, the philosophical and the political wove a seamless whole in an active, questing and pioneering life. In this sense she was also a hierophant, a teacher who "shows forth", taking the mysteries from the secret temple to function in the wider world.

Sapientia Sapiente Dono Data—"Wisdom is a gift given to the Wise"—was Farr's Golden Dawn motto. Like the Ouroborus symbol of Wisdom, the serpent swallowing its tail, Farr's life, though still progressive, had come full circle. In earlier years, Florence had attended the first college for the higher education of girls in London and had tried her hand at teaching; in the last years of her life she was a teacher and administrator at Ceylon's first school for girls.

Florence Farr's contribution to the modern magical and mystical corpus is immense. Her original and refreshing output is only now becoming fully recognised as she moves into the magical spotlight from the long shadows cast by her companions Yeats and Shaw.

Florence Farr was an adept. Not just in title, bestowed by S.L. Mathers as "Chief Adept in Anglia" of the Golden Dawn. The twin streams of magic and mysticism were balanced in her, like the double serpents of the caduceus wand. She carried the spirit of enquiry and experiment, always with perfect integrity. She studied hard for her magic, and believed that "to accept a ready-made belief blindly is to commit mental and moral suicide."

The scope of Farr's magical exploration and understanding is impressive. It is surprising that it has been hidden in plain sight for so long. The writings and the battles of the male magicians of the Hermetic Order of the Golden Dawn are well known, the women only now coming into the light as serious contenders. Florence Farr is becoming better known thanks to the work of

Darcy Küntz and others such as Josephine Johnson and Mary Greer. The body of Farr's occult writing gathered here speaks for itself; however, I think she will become recognised as one of the most significant and important magicians to have come from The Hermetic Order of the Golden Dawn.

In *Egyptian Magic* she says:

> "Now Isis was a Woman knowing Words of Magical Power, her heart was weary of multitudes of men, and she chose the multitude of Gods, but above all the multitude of the Shining Ones. And she meditated in her heart and said 'Might not I, also, by means of the names of Shining Power become as the Sun God in Heaven?'"

This quote from the *Egyptian Book of the Dead*, which in *Egyptian Magic* Florence calls "the Triumphant Death-song of the Initiated Egyptian", is apt here: "I fly up to heaven and I alight upon earth and mine eye turneth back towards the traces of my footsteps. I am the offspring of yesterday. The caverns of the earth have given me birth, and I am revealed at my appointed time."

Thanks to Darcy Küntz for compiling this great collection, which will be invaluable to scholars, historians and magicians.

CAROLINE WISE,
London, 2012.

The Magic of a Symbol

by Florence Farr

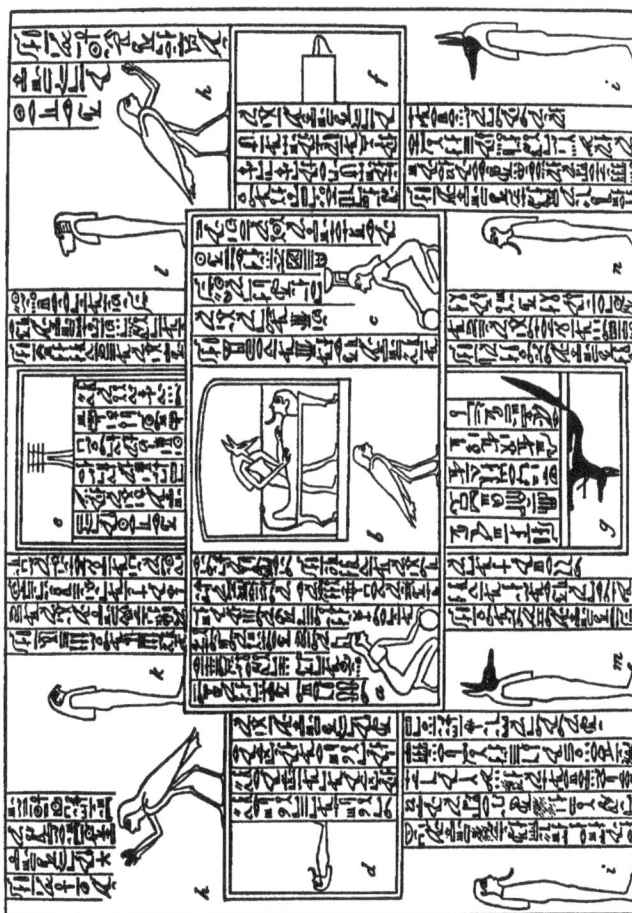

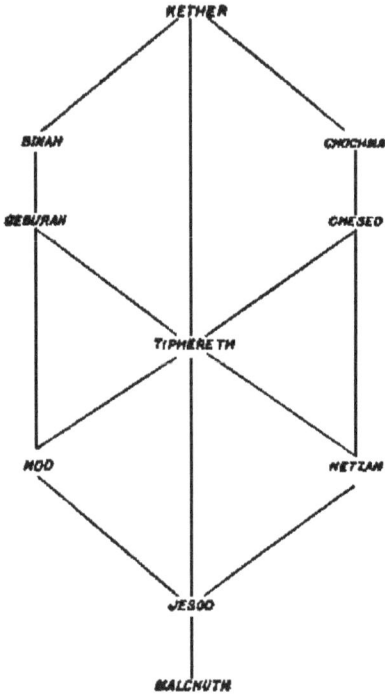

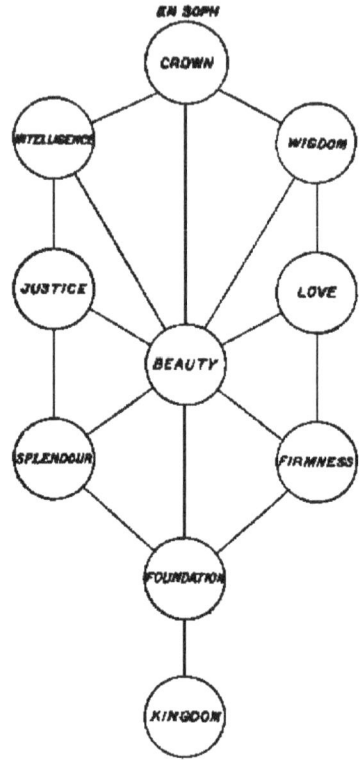

Kenneth Mackenzie's Tree of Life
The Royal Masonic Cyclopaedia, (1877)

The Magic of a Symbol

by Florence Farr

2012
GOLDEN DAWN RESEARCH TRUST

The Magic of a Symbol was first published in 1996 by Holmes Publishing Group, USA as part of the *Golden Dawn Studies Series, No.* 6.

This revised edition was published by The Golden Dawn Research Trust in 2012.

The cover page illustration 'The Coffin Chamber' is from E.A. Wallis Budge's *The Mummy*. New Jersey, 1989.

The God-forms of the Golden Dawn's Neophyte Grade are based upon this illustration.

Contents

The Magic of a Symbol[1]

THE Japanese, who keep only one beautiful object in each room, know the reward of limiting sense impressions and giving the imagination time to work with the impression it has received. This same reward arises from the use of symbols, for to the mind each impression is a possible symbol of unimagined magnificence. A line of verse, a piece of inlay, may easily sink so deep into the substance of thought that it can take root and grow, for that is the meaning of culture. So we give our impressions time to grow into trees, that ideas, like birds, may come and sit in their branches.

When the ancients used symbols as objects of meditation they knew this reward given to simple impressions; and I have found that the use of symbols restores to the mind a forgotten power of concentration. They force us to think about a given thing for a considerable period of time and make it impossible to carry on two or three trains of thought at once. They help us to watch our minds at work. If we focus the attention on a symbol we can recall the whole train of imagination and ideas that arise from the symbolic root. In trying to still thought without the use of a symbol the task is still harder, for then irrelevant ideas arise and pass in fantastic pantomime before the eye of the mind, or the memory revolves on some familiar topic in fruitless iteration.

If we focus the attention consecutively on two different symbols we can compare our moods under the different stimuli, for the symbol will give a stimulus towards a mood if it is allowed time to do so. More than this, we can experiment, we can criticize and compare our feelings, when we fix our attention and call up any images without reference to ancient tradition. Or we can use the tradition and, as the ancients did, imagine or regard the symbol of a hawk's eye with the intention of bringing the mind in contact with the keen sight of the bird that can gaze at the sun without dismay.

Again, we might not only wish for sight but for actual power of imagining ourselves to take on characteristics alien to our nature. I am told a great majority of people cannot use their imagination in thinking at all. They cannot sympathize or feel with other creatures or people of different temperaments from their own; they cannot act or pretend to feel what they do not feel; they cannot see what others are like enough even to make a caricature of them. Many people can never describe a person or an event in words, and very often they cannot even express their own thoughts. These people have vague feelings of attraction or repulsion, but no impression that they can express accurately. They are, like the elementary substance, capable of irritation, but not capable of ideas or the expression of ideas. This is partly because of the modern spirit, which demands repletion of every sense and overfeeding both of the mind and body. They do not understand art because they look it too many pictures, or religion because they go to church too often, or music because they attend too many concerts.

When we realize what this state of mind means we do all we can to try and acquire the power of transformation which is above all things necessary to us if our life is to be a human life and not the life of an animal. We must learn to feel with others and to understand them. The Egyptians called the Lord of this discipline of the mind, Kephera, the Transformer. His symbol is the sun at midnight and the scarab. By reducing the mind to the peacefulness of the darkest hour of the night, by sinking into a state in which we for a time forget the eternal "I am" we learn to understand the deeper strata of our "Being."

The wise student who wishes to attain the power and

understanding of transformation approaches that realm where the absolute and the relative are seen to be co-existent aspects of the one Being; where the consciousness symbolized by the mathematical point, aware of its unity of substance with all other points, is realized as the ultimate state of all Being, apart from moods and tenses. At the same time all egoisms are perceived to be arrangements of this substance, or rather ideas created by the notion of separateness and form. The symbols of lines, surfaces, solids and spaces are modes or arrangements of these ultimate points. They symbolize consciousness extended in certain directions and drawn in from others.

The use of symbols as a means of focusing the mind and as a means of perceiving abstruse ideas is only touched upon now because all the mystics used them in these ways, as will be pointed out in detail later on.

Let us consider now what we have to take the place of symbols. For it is certain that very few of this generation have ever tried to discipline their thoughts in any way. Sometimes a man here and there becomes aware of the folly of his revolving memory and his wild imaginations, and his only remedy is work. Incessant work silences the folly of thought; but it silences the wisdom of thought also. Why does he not try the effect of wise and ordered thought, and study the structure of his mind? Is it because of the terror that confronts him on the threshold of this adventure? The terror of responsibility?

Most of us will choose any alternative rather than sit still and think until we see clearly as the sun itself that we alone are responsible for what we are. The weight of that terror makes us fly to work, to pleasure, to anything that will crowd our minds with irrelevant things. A man will cover up his own sanctuary with a veil and worship any other god; he will attend ceremonies; he will adore before many altars, but he will not listen to the inner voice. Any other responsibility he will accept, fatherhood, the government of people, the command in battle, but not the responsibility for himself. Or he laughs at life, and reproaches God with his misfortunes. Like Omar he says:

> O thou who didst with pitfall and with gin
> Beset the path I was to wander in,
> For all the sin wherewith the face of man
> Is blackened—man's forgiveness give and take.

"Why was this life of misery ever contrived?" We ask; and those of us who have listened for the answer hear the reply quite clearly: "Because you yourself wearied of the unchangeable bliss of infinite Being, and voluntarily separated yourself in order that the spectacle of life might pass in a panorama before your eyes; you were so enamoured of those phantasies that you have almost forgotten whence you came and the way of return is hard to find." When we have heard this answer, we see the reason of many things, and we no longer think life so worthy of reproach.

Then we search for the source of responsible cause, and we watch its first movements as relativity in time and space and growth. We seek for the stable point in Time and find it Now; the stable point in Space and find it Here; the stable point in growth and creation and we find it This. This Here and Now exist everywhere, at all times and under all conditions. The eternal paradox is hidden in these words, for they are ever different but ever present, and both these things together. In the midst of change they subsist as the roots of changing form. The roots of the World-Tree, growth and decay, past and future, form and name, can be concentrated into these three points of This, Here, Now. After all, the World-Tree is a wonderful thing. Why should we not sit among the roots of it with the ancient sages and Death, the Lord of gods? For we are one with them, and it is because we have eaten of the Tree that we forget that we are ourselves That which gave it birth.

When we accept the responsibility wisdom will come, for it is given as a gift to the wise. When we arise from our illusions and watch deep in our own hearts the inveterate notions of Time and Space and Cause which are the necessities of our ways of thinking, we see them crouching in their lairs waiting to spring out on us or to steal gently and lead us down the long roads which have no ending, and we begin to understand the impostors we so long have harboured as our ideals. Progress is the name of the arch-illusionist, for it is the serpent which tempts us to look ever onward and beyond, instead of waking to the fullest realization here and now. The Utmost and the Highest are within us now if we will but look within and find the great secret of community of Being. But no, the mind refuses to believe it; it desires stimulus for action, it wants to have more, to do more, to be more. It delights in the ebb and flow of change and apparent progress.

Our meditations on real Being may be assisted by the use of mathematical symbols, such as cubes, tetrads, lines, circles, points. For as Leonardo da Vinci says: "Believe nothing till you can reduce it to a mathematical formulary." And mathematical symbols are a great comfort to the searcher after True Being.

But this is only a part of the work of symbols. If they can be a focus for the imagination, they can also be a focus for the will, and they are used by some who desire to awaken their latent powers in order to concentrate attention on the work to be accomplished.

That most mysterious of all moods, the mood of Faith, flourishes sometimes when it is, as it were, watered by the daily recollection of the imagination. And the imagination may be helped by the use of some moving symbol. The wise teacher sometimes uses symbols, just as the priest unveils the symbols of religion before his people that they may receive an influx of the enthusiasm that awakens the potent mood of faith. There are many other times when symbols such as a flag are of enormous value in conveying emotion to a regiment. A crowd is moved by a pageant and by the sight of some representation of dramatic goodness, badness, or heroism. A conjuror acts in the same way and uses symbols with which he is familiar to cast a glamour over the little group of people he is about to delude. And I was told by a young chela [or pupil] that his master had taught him the means of counteracting the symbols used by the jugglers, so that he might not be deceived by the tricks they performed.

These are a few of the uses that have been made of symbols. But I want specially to talk of them as a help to the understanding of our own mystery, and in thinking of magic do not let us associate it with the foolishness of the present age, but rather go back to the real meaning of the word. Magic power only implies a power not limited by common experience, neither is the painting of great pictures nor the writing of great books limited by common experience. Both these things can be achieved only by two or three men in a generation. Magic power was a power given as a gift to those who had diligently set themselves to the work of understanding. "What is this phantom being I call myself?" What mystical Cup is the fountain of its being?

The human soul is very hard to find, very hard even to symbolize, so hard that most of us have given up the quest. It hides from us under fantastic disguises. It appears to one man as his passions, to another as his curiosity, to another as his conscience, to another as his faith. To a few it is known as the source of all these things; and they symbolize it as a fountain or cup.

The creative [or *Briah*] world of the Kabbalah is symbolized by a cup. The crater, the bowl, the cauldron are all symbolic of plenitude and fecundity. The Quest of the Holy Grail has woven itself into English literature for hundreds of years. Persian mystics interpret the cup to mean the skull, the seat of the imagination; and the wine it contains is the inebriation of the spirit which is the fourth state of mystic meditation.

The Gnostics write of the cup of oblivion given to the souls of men before birth that they may forget their true state; they write also of the cup of wisdom given to the good in order that they may not forget.[2]

According to the Vedanta Philosophy the cup of ignorance (Avidya) is the source of man's separated life. It is the *Karana Sharira* (creative soul) of a human being, while the creative soul of a god is Mâyâ, the cup of wisdom (vidya or mâyâ). For the Divine Being is aware of the deceptive nature of form in the same way as a skilled juggler is aware that his hands are creating delusion deceptive to his own eyes. But the soul who creates a man enters into his creation, is deluded as it were by his own handiwork, and in this way separates himself by pride from wisdom and enters into ignorance.

Hence there are two cups, the holy cup of Sophia and the profane cup of folly, and on this point the Gnostics and Vedantists are agreed.

According to Hermes Trismegistus the cup or monad is the cup of unity. The initiate plunged his body into the cup of the mind. Baptism is this symbolic plunging of the whole nature into the mind-filled font. In the state of fulfilment called the Pleroma the mind and body are unified in a subtilized body and heaven and earth are mixed therein. The earliest words alluding to the sacramental feast of bread and wine are to be found on the walls of the Pyramid of Unas at Sakara, date about 3700 B.C. The children of the sun were Shu and Tefnut, the divine twin boy and girl. He was symbolized by the white wheaten bread and she by the drink made from the red barley. Her name means the height of the sky whence the Elixir of Life descended upon earth as from an inverted bowl at noon-time. His name meant the light of dawn, and he stands holding up his hands as the separator of light and darkness. As we shall see presently under another symbolic formula he is the Doer, she the Eye of Light or Seer, and these two together are the elements of the cross.

For the present, however, we must keep to our quest of the cup. The next place in which we find it is on some old playing cards called the tarot. These are divining cards and differ a good deal from modern playing cards. The four suits are wands, cups, swords and pentacles, taking the place of diamonds, hearts, spades and clubs. They had somewhat the same symbols among the ancient Irish, who called them the spear, the cauldron, the sword, and the stone. They symbolize fire, water, air and earth; also energy, love, intellect and the physical body. They have been associated with the Tetragrammaton of the Kabbalists, and the worlds of [*Atziluth* or] archetype, [*Briah* or] creation, [*Yetzirah* or] formation and [*Assiah* or] matter. So that we come to the idea of Eve and creation symbolized by the cups or hearts of playing cards. It is only a year or two ago that the relationship between the suits of cups and hearts appeared in the vision of a seer who imagined his consciousness to enter into a symbolic chamber in the region of the heart and found therein a palace with porphyry pillars and lamps formed like serpents with jewelled lights in their heads and a man holding a cup in his right hand.

In a Vedantic book called the *Yoga Vasishta Laghu* the states of the seeker are divided into seven degrees, and in the last but one the soul is compared to water in a vessel floating in the ocean but protected from the disturbance of storms and tides. The holy man in this degree has made a sanctuary for his soul, a closed place in which he may hold converse with his Being. In the final stage of meditation this vessel is broken, and the soul, which has found its true nature in the cup of holy peace, must remember the truth when it is cast without refuge into the ocean of changing life. In this symbolism the cup serves as a means to an end, for in the state of peaceful meditation the silence is full of ecstasy. It is the cup of the elixir which strengthens the tired soul on its pilgrimage. Like the mythical walled city of gold it is a refuge from the turmoil of change and corruption. But the supreme adventure must be attempted sooner or later, and the soul must resolve to remember always whether doing good or evil, whether seeing beauty or ugliness, that its immortality depends upon its unity with the master of illusion instead of with the slave of illusion. In other words its immortality depends upon its capacity for understanding its own immortal substance. Its substance is eternal, but is not always aware of its own Being, because it is too much aware of its own qualities.

I have already said that it is possible to discipline the mind by the use of symbols used as a focus for the imagination. Let us contemplate a method of this nature.

The devout student has chosen, let us say, the symbol of the Holy Grail. He finds among his treasures an ancient crystal cup and sets it in a shrine. Here when the world is at peace, perhaps in the early hours before dawn, he lights a lamp, burning some sweet smelling oil, and swings his thurible of incense slowly to and fro. The first degree of the work is to collect the wandering thoughts and fix the whole power of the intellect upon the symbol of his meditation; the second degree is attained when his body has become unwilling to stir; soon afterwards the sense of quietude pervades the whole mind and body. Later on, the mind reaches the fourth degree and becomes inebriated with the store of life gathered into it. It is as if the stilling of the flow of thought had turned the wine into a fire of burning spirit, filling the cup of sacrifice. The fifth degree is the absolute stilling of all thoughts and images, and the symbol is forgotten in the great expanses of formless exultation. The sixth is the degree of privation; terror and anguish attend the pilgrim as he is passing to the higher degrees of consciousness. Pride is the gate which shuts him out from these; pride in his own powers and attainments and limitations. For the essence of individuality is pride; and the desire to keep distinguishing characteristics is pride. So the sixth degree is one of trembling and fear. It may take years and centuries to pass through this gate, but all of a sudden it opens, and the flooding in of wider consciousness is known. This is the seventh degree. The cup is filled with the Elixir of Enlightenment, and he has seen the Holy Grail. The man who has reached this stage is henceforth an illuminated being and will gradually reap the fruits of illumination in his daily life.

After the seventh degree is reached a great veil must be passed before the real mysteries of the Trinity in Unity can be understood. But long before this the man has analysed the Trinity in his own heart, and he has learned to look upon his substance as an ocean and his mind as the waves that traverse it. The cup has taught him to understand that in the last degree each particle is similar to all particles, and the diversity of the waves is the relation of the particles one to the other. The sense of relation or germ of intellectual comparison is the Great Mother Understanding. Her symbol is the Dove, carrying messages to and fro, the messenger which governs intellectual movements and defines the relation between one part and another. The origin of intellect is a definition of relation between the parts of the whole. Directly duality became possible a trinity became inevitable. When the two perceive each other comparison and relation arise as a third.

The last three degrees of meditation are mingled with these unspeakably tenuous ideas of ultimate unity. In the eighth degree the soul merges into the divine triad, the root of intellect, and becomes unified with the contemplated symbol; it itself is the Grail or container of the Divine Understanding; this is called the degree of ecstasy. The ninth degree of rapture is called the Divine Espousals, because the soul perceives its own absolute nature; the cup disappears and the separated nature passes into the unified nature leaving the soul in the simple absolute state which can perceive no differences; this is the tenth degree. The cup and the fire of love which melted it alike disappear. The virgin soul purified of all taint is crowned. This coronation of the Virgin is called by some the Divine Marriage because henceforward the soul cannot forget the nature of its ultimate state.

On the return from a meditation in which these ten degrees, have been passed the soul experiences first rapture, then ecstasy, before its return to ordinary consciousness. It then becomes aware of a widely extended consciousness in which all things created and uncreated have a part. With anguish it sinks back into the individual state and passes through the degrees of peace, inebriation and quietude, and then once more aware of its body and the circumstances of its life meekly closes the shrine which contains the symbol of its blessedness and passes out into the world we live in.

In this example I have carefully compared the mystical theology of the Catholic Church and the Kabbalistic degrees of the ten Sephiroth, and I think both these doctrines have been founded on the experiences of sane and accredited mystics. Scaramelli's book gives the process in far greater detail, and it has received the sanction of the Church of Rome.

There are other methods of using symbols to make impressions on our senses. For instance, the crucifix made with an oval centre and limbs like a Maltese cross but with one prolonged as in the modern crucifix, appears in the carving on the walls of the Pyramid at Sakara, dating nearly 4000 B.C. It is used as a determinative for the word Nedz which is translated into Greek Soter, or saviour. The later form of the hieroglyph is an upright pole with twisted cords forming the cross-beam. Egyptologists translate it "avenger," and it is applied to the son who avenges or saves his father from destruction. Horus is the great type of this work, and he saves his father Osiris from

Set, his evil brother, who had put him to death and scattered his limbs throughout the land of Egypt. This crucifix was only used in the very early times in this relation, so that it is interesting that it should have emerged again three thousand years later as an emblem for the same redemptive idea in the symbology of the Christian Church.

EGYPTIAN DAD.

NEDZ (LATER FORM).

NEDZ (EARLY FORM, 4000 B.C.).

The teachers of mankind who understood the value of association of ideas usually added the story of some popular myth to the symbol they intended to use, so that the sight of the symbol awakened the memory of the myth, and a hieratic allegory was later on constructed round the same symbol and communicated as the secret meaning to the initiated. It is true that to enjoin secrecy is one of the most effectual ways of impressing the memory, and the natural mind delights in analogy and will indulge in it as a fascinating pastime. It gives it a false sense of understanding the infinite; but it is very often a limitation to the real growth of the imagination. A priesthood which sets itself to weave folk stories into the ritual of religion gains great skill in working out analogies and uses the emblems of ideas it has woven into a discreet and orderly pattern to awaken the emotions and rouse the sleeping powers of the adolescents and sensitives under the discipline of its colleges.

CALVARY OR LATIN CROSS   GREEK CROSS AND CIRCLE.   THE EGYPTIAN AUNK.
AND CIRCLE.

The early cross was the symbol of the victorious Horus. He had fought with Set, the cruel brother of Osiris, the beautiful one. Set in some way represented activity and generation and Horus the sight of the seer. The result of the fight was that both gods were maimed, for it was no longer possible for Horus to see or for Set to generate. The blind Horus, however, was declared victorious and his sight restored. The Egyptians studied the art of self-control, and the first and most intimate enemy of self-control is the teeming mind which pours a stream of images before the vision. This must be sterilized by the seer resolutely closing his eyes to vision of any kind, and then Osiris rewards him by instructing him in the secret of his own liberation.

Another form of the cross called the Ankh, or symbol of Life, is found among the pottery marks of the first dynasty, and may date from the hypothetical age of Osiris himself, five or six thousand years before Christ.[3]

The oldest form of the *Ankh* is the head of a man with the arms outstretched; but the hands are uplifted on either side of the face, in the attitude Moses assumed when he desired the children of Israel might overcome their enemies in battle. It is curious that these uplifted arms also represent the active part of the soul, or Ka, in the symbolic system of Egypt. The symbol of a head represents Horus—or Hru, as his name was spelt in Egypt—and the upright pillar was the *Dad*, or symbol of Osiris. It is called the backbone of Osiris and was associated with the practices of meditation on the minute central passage in the spinal cord.

We can analyse the symbol of life as a figure of a human being uniting the three elements represented by Horus, Osiris and Set. The head is Horus, the arms Set, and the body Osiris.

The body is the symbol of the idea of the Logos, or Name, the word Dad, and in the Pyramid texts we find it written out in full. It is identical with the word for "saying," "speech," or "Logos." Sometimes it is called the Tower of Flame or the blasting furnace-tower of Set-Hor. The Speech, or Osiris, united to the active generative power of Set and the insight of Horus, are the elements in the Egyptian cross or symbol of Life.

These three can be developed by training. Generation, becomes a power when it and its counterpart, imagination, are illuminated into the mystery of faith, for then there is a transubstantiation of the flesh. It rises in a great tidal wave and casts down all the closed gates and breaks the frame of the mind, so that the man becomes more than human. Thereafter no human law can measure his good and his evil, for it does not belong to the world of men. This wonderful and dangerous power of faith is one of the secrets that have always been guarded, but some of our geniuses have achieved it and some of our madmen have been shattered by it. Whence it comes or whither its goes cannot be told. Speech, in the same way, becomes a power when it is inspired and breathes beauty as an atmosphere to sense; for the word *Unnoufer*, the title of Osiris, means "beautiful being"; and he is the symbol of all beauty, and the Dionysian enthusiasm was the enthusiasm for the wine of Osiris, the spirit of beauty. Beauty is most active when she is enthroned in nature and awakens intuition and the love which covers a multitude of sins. Finally sight, as Horus, is the symbol of wisdom, the eternal watcher, and under the ancient symbols of the gods Set, Osiris and Horus we perceive the whole symbol of Life to contain the three ways of the great ones: imagination and the arts and works; beauty and the qualities of perfection; insight, wisdom and philosophy.

The cross and circle have been handed down to us in various relations. Let us imagine the circle to mean insight and wisdom, the upright pole the Beautiful Being and the cross-beam to mean creation. Then let us interpret the progress typified by the change from the circle surmounting the cross shaped like the letter T, to the circle in the centre of a calvary cross and finally to the Greek cross surrounded by a circle. In the first instance the head, as a circle, symbolizes the wheel of the mind circling among the senses; in the second instance the wheel of the mind is centred in the region of the heart and the ideal of beautiful Being has reached upward to the head; the cross-bar also springs from the heart. We see in this change, the ritual of a spiritual progress in which the frame of the mind is broken and intuition, insight and imaginative faith satisfy the desire for instruction by words and experience, by vision and by works of generation. Dionysos has visited a man when he has passed through the telestic rites and unified the moods of his soul. Afterwards when the symbol is changed to the equal-armed cross within the circle a man learns the unity of the worlds and the circle of wisdom surrounds the equal armed cross of beauty and imagination. In the centre of the earth which is the mystical omphalos, man has become united with nature and woven himself into the web of her various existences. He has found the symbol of the stone of the wise and realized its power in his own person.

In these changing crosses we must notice that the generative power of the imagination symbolized by the cross-bar passes from the place of the head to the heart and finally to the mystical omphalos; while the circle of wisdom passes from the head to the heart and finally outward till it surrounds the whole; and the beautiful Being alone remains unchanged in the midst. So Osiris, being perfect in himself, remains the same, suffering the migrations of the two divine combatants Set and Horus. And Set, who rose up against him and hid him from the world in the storms of generative excess, is reduced through faith and devotion, or the way of the heart, to Being, or the way of the midst, the point of balance. Horus, by interchange of wisdom and imagination, is for a time blinded by the combat, but afterwards gains the perfect victory and becomes the boundary of the fullness of divine life.

The Hierophants of the ancient mysteries, as I said before, delighted in these analogies and in the cruder analogies of puns and accidental resemblances which often appear to us quite meaningless unless we are willing to take a symbol into our own hearts and meditate upon it until it grows into a tree of life.

Notes:
1. 'The Magic of a Symbol,' was originally printed in *The Occult Review*, Vol. VII: No. 2. London: William Rider & Son Ltd., February 1908. pp. 82-93.—D.K.
2. *Fragments of a Faith Forgotten*, Mead, p. 518.—F.F.
3. *Royal Tombs of First Dynasty*, by Flinders Petrie.—F.F.

Egyptian Use of Symbols[1]

So many books have been published lately on the history, customs and religions of Egypt that I shall not attempt to say anything about the facts of the case. Any one who cares to take the trouble can read about them elsewhere. What we want to do in order to get into touch with ancient Egypt is to imagine ourselves belonging to a nation that believed in the immortality of the soul and acted up to its belief.

The Egyptians believed everything that Europeans believe; but their faith was so great that it influenced their conduct in their public life and in their private relations.

The great believed that they literally were the sons of gods, for their fathers had invoked the god and had performed rites and made meditations and imagined overshadowings of divine natures before they were conceived. Marriage was a sacrament of most momentous nature involving long purifications and the communion with the Divine Trinities of Mother, Father and Child. Death was the consummation of initiation, and the regeneration of the body literally meant that the great initiates among them did believe that they could "take on" the forms of the soul at will and manifest to their representatives on earth in some shadowy substance whenever they desired to do so.

The descendants of the King offered sacrifices of living animals and fruits and wines on the days of the funeral; but they knew that thereafter the symbols or representations of these things would be sufficient for the purpose of the departed one. The kings had words written on the walls of their tombs telling of what had been offered to their subtle bodies (*Ka*); and they presented statues and pictures for the subtle body to permeate. The sensitive standing before such a statue and gazing into its eyes while he made offering to the manes of his ancestor seemed to see the form breathe and move while in his heart he knew the will of the great ancestor whose spirit had found union with the Superman Osiris. We offer flowers on the graves of our dead, but we do not communicate with them in our hearts; and the Egyptians did not do so either, unless the dead man or woman was an initiate who had learned to unite his powers and manifest upon earth or in the underworld at will.

The initiated Egyptian believed death involved the separation of the principles which united during incarnation to make an individual man. The rhythm of life and death appeared as a rhythm of union and separation. The will, appearing periodically as a compelling star, presided over birth and death, then faded back into the ether which was its substance. Under its influence, which was symbolized by the sun, a reflection arose symbolized by the moon, and together these powers formed the manifestation from the symbols of earth and air.

Ra, the sun, was the wine and sacrament, and Osiris, the earth, was the bread, and they united between the pillars of fire and cloud. Osiris was the lord of the underworld, opening and closing the gates of its separate chambers that Ra might pass through with the train of gods. And the idea of the initiate was that he should become one with Osiris, and make his manifestation on earth or climb up the ladder of heaven at will. The ladder was another symbol of the pillars. Set and Horus stood on either side of it, and when the initiate took an upward step he was united to Set, and when he stood upright on the step he was united to Horus. All this sounds very confusing, and it is still more confusing if read in the translations now obtainable. The only possible way of arriving at the solution of this symbolism is to apply it to the processes going on in the mental world. Every day we pass through all possible phases of consciousness. Broadly speaking they are deep sleep or unconsciousness; dreaming or thinking subjectively, without special reference to actions; and thinking and acting objectively or with regard to our surroundings and what we call facts. Deep sleep may be unconscious or it may develop into what has been called luminous sleep, or the heavenly state. The ladder which enables a man to reach the heaven world, or luminous sleep, is straight and narrow. By great will power, or concentration of the attention, it is possible to keep the balance between Horus and Set; that is to say, between the immortal fighters in the mind, which make the attention fall into an oblivious state or into the ceaseless wanderings of ordinary cogitation. These immortal fighters represent the subjective consciousness and the state of deep sleep. The inexperienced mind is always either wandering or unconscious; it has to fill itself with experience before it can watch and compare and harmonize the two states. When it has done so it realizes that in deep sleep or trance it is in a creative state, and prepares new combinations of its elements, and in the subjective state it is formulating these combinations and giving them definite form as thoughts. It is in the state called heavenly or luminous sleep that these things can be perceived. The man knows that he is one with his Creator and accepts the responsibility of that tremendous power. He becomes one with the Sun God in heaven; then with his train of creative powers he visits the *Duat*, or Underworld, which is the subjective world, or world of dream. Here he will find all the powers of the mental world, all the dreams and memories of the past, and all the plans and hopes for the future. It is a workshop where the drama is prepared that will be acted upon earth.

The great difference between the earth and the *Duat* must be sought for in the difference between the physical life and the life of the mind. In the mind, or world of the *Duat*, the actor studies his part, he plans it, he consults with the creator or author, he receives impressions; in the physical world the play is produced, and the audience is impressed favourably or unfavourably. Manifestation of ideas takes place in visible form.

In Egypt the gods were everywhere worshipped, but the initiate was one with the gods. They represented the powers of the man who had realized that, by sacrifice of the little self, the great self was to be attained. This tremendous ideal is not a popular one. Innumerable seekers after truth recoil before the idea of losing their own individuality in the individuality of a perfect being. They would rather keep their own limitations than merge themselves in the unlimited.

It is just as if a drop of water desired to remain for ever suspended as dew on the petals of a flower. It is separated, and it would rather evaporate in its struggle to keep its separate life than fall into the stream that is hurrying past to join the great ocean of consciousness. But I think we do not understand the nature of consciousness when we feel in this way. The Egyptians did.

Osiris represented to them the ocean of Human Consciousness, *Ra* the ocean of Cosmic Consciousness; and they realized that to enter into these beings was to attain plenitude and not to suffer deprivation. An individual consciousness as we know it is a partial consciousness. The subjective world has deprived itself of the consciousness of everything it calls the objective world. I am myself because I am different from all people and things I can see around me. I am inferior to some and worship them by my love or envy; I am superior to others and pity them by my love or pride; and there are a very few whom I can look upon as real companions and comrades. In the same way with possessions, some are too good, some too bad and some are obtainable. Now this clinging to individuality is the great delusion which makes us so fatally interested in the state of being, as we are at present, mere aggregations of particles which are as aggregations incapable of immortality.

The moment we look at the question from outside we realize we should not like the present state of things to last for ever. It is amusing to play the game, to pretend for a little while that we feel deeply about this or that; but directly we put it to the test and say to ourselves, "Do I want such and such a thing not only for a lifetime but for ever?" We know very well we could not endure it. In our hearts we know that the charm of life is that it is ceaselessly changing. Even those who know the feeling of liberation from the delusion of delight in their own individuality, those who have lain down as Osiris, and entered into the shrine of Ra, even those will not seek the liberation of eternal contemplation. They cannot tear themselves away from the wheel of existence; they return, they say, to help the ignorant and guide the steps of the helpless. The wheel of change fascinates them; and the gods are delighted by the drama that ceaselessly unrolls itself before them. This was what the Egyptians felt. Deep in the centre of the world of the *Duat*, in the navel of the wheel, dwelt Seker, the god who never moved. He had finished his course, and Ra cried to him at midnight, when his boat was towed within hearing of his abode in the depths of the Underworld.

Seker answered the cry of *Ra*, but none ever looked upon his face. In later times Osiris was shown in the form of a mummified hawk and was called *Ptah-Seker-Osiris*, and the supreme mystery of the adepts was hidden under this symbol.

The mummified body fixed for ever in its eternal dwelling was the symbol of that central immovable point round which all changing things revolve. The illumination of the creative

Sun-God passing through the great hierarchies of creation symbolized by the signs of the Zodiac was the wheel of Ptah, the opener or beginner of creation and the circle of the wheel. Osiris, the human being who had joined the alpha and omega of creation and passed from one to the other at will, represented the human desire to attain peace eternal, ameliorated by the possibility of change, even if it were merely the wheel of perpetual recurrence symbolized by the changing seasons of the year. So Osiris is crucified on the spokes of the wheel in order that his consciousness may extend into the world of relative consciousness, or retire into the place of absolute consciousness at will. And the name of *Ptah-Seker-Osiris* was the symbol of this power of the human adept.

Notes:
1. 'Egyptian Use of Symbols,' was originally printed in *The Occult Review*, Vol. VII: No. 3. London: William Rider & Son Ltd., March 1908. pp. 146-149.—D.K.

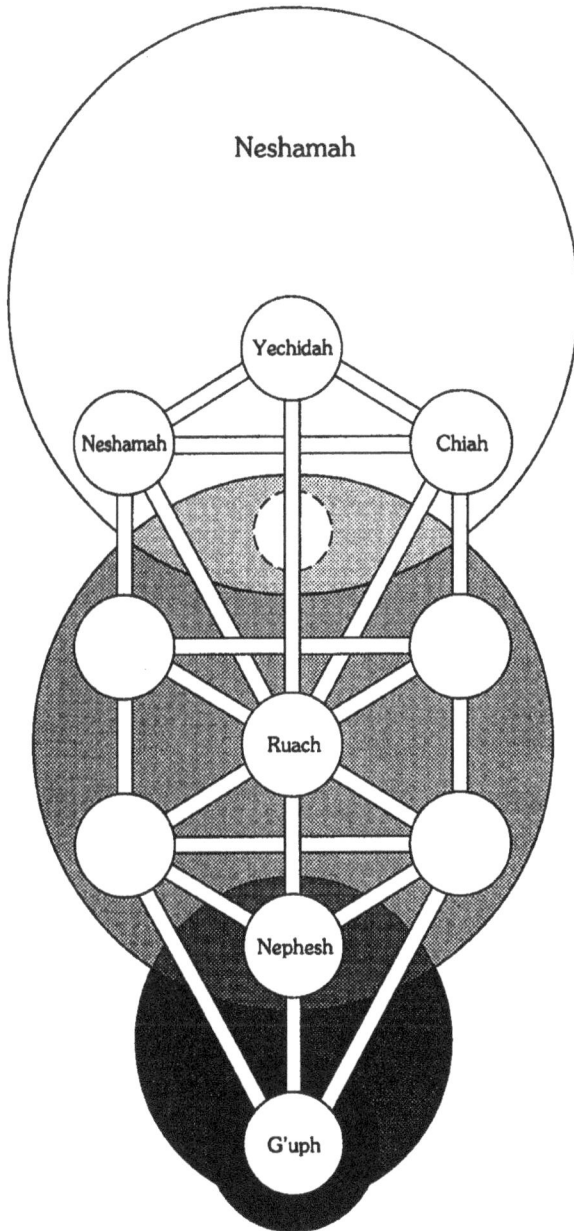

Parts of the Soul on the Tree of Life
Chic and Tabatha Cicero *Self-Initiation Into the
Golden Dawn Tradition*, (2002)

On the Kabbalah[1]

THE mind is orderly and it revels in the law of correspondence, and the Kabbalah is perhaps the most elaborate revel the mind of man has ever held. The letters of the alphabet were systematized in the worlds of number and sound. Each represented number and an idea, and the numerals themselves were arrangements, or qualities, or hierarchies, or worlds formed from the division of ideal unity.

Preceding number were the three states of negative existence, corresponding to the state of a seed. These are called Nothingness [*Ain*]–Unlimitedness [*Ain Soph*]–and Limitless Light [*Ain Soph Aur*].

The ten first numbers are attributed to ten divine qualities, ten archangels, ten hierarchies, ten worlds and innumerable demonic beings and worlds. The six first numbers are arranged at the corners of a hexagram, the four last in a Calvary cross. I will not go further into details of the correspondence of the ten numbers, for the four letters of the Holy Name must now be woven into the four worlds, and the ten Sephiroth multiplied into forty, each world corresponding to an element and a plane.

It was possible to reduce every number from one to forty to its exact correspondence and equivalent; and not only this but every letter of the Hebrew alphabet carried the same symbolism after another manner. It was all stately and elaborate, and in an Appendix I have given more details of the ideas connected with it and one plate from the rare fourth volume of Rosenroth's *Kabbalah* [*Unveiled*].[2] But in this place I will only speak of the kind of symbolism such a system implies.

If it were founded on some tangible correspondence, such as the chemist, Mendelejeff's *Periodic Law*, it is easy to see that it would be the key to the rhythm of physical and mental states. We can imagine a thread of memory carrying our consciousness back to the ultimate unity of the first Sephirah and emerging from that into the complexity of physical life by elaborate and coherent arrangements of particles. The ultimate structure of atoms may very probably be revealed eventually as following some definite law of the kind as elaborately repeated in more and more complex patterns as the temperature is reduced. If so, one who has studied the details of the Kabbalistic system as described in the works of Reuchlin and Pico della Mirandola will be able to apply the principles he has learned to the actual facts of science. He will have no difficulty in admitting that the root of mind and body are both to be found in the simple states of prima materia. The thread of memory will carry him from the Form to the Formless, and he will realize the possibility of passing to and fro from the material [or *Assiah*] to the formative [or *Yetzirah*], from the formative to the creative [or *Briah*], and from the creative to the archetypal [or *Atziluth*] worlds, in an elaborate gymnastic of the mind. The body is the Garden of Eden and the Tree of Life in the midst are the ten Sephiroth. They are the key of life also and are arranged, in the form of a circle surmounting a cross, not unlike the symbol of the planet Venus.

The symbol may be taken to represent the aureole of forces surrounding the man within the man. We read of this Being in the Upanishads as the man in the heart, the size of a thumb. He is the conscious Being within us and can move from place to place by an effort of attention. The configuration of the Sephiroth shows the relative stations of the Universal and the Individual, and the interplay of the internal and the external life breaths or Sephiroth.

I think enough has been said to show that Jacob Boehme and William Blake were inspired by the same desire to construct a system of correspondences as the elaborators of the Kabbalah. It is a kind of revel of the mind, of no interest to any one who has not become obsessed by the idea of construction. I do not think that the Kabbalistic system works, but I believe the Jews lament this and attribute it to the loss of the Word which legend says was stolen from the Temple.

We still have traces of the old methods of divination by means of the Kabbalah in our playing cards, and more especially in the Tarot pack of seventy-eight cards, which consists of groups exactly corresponding to the symbols of the Kabbalah.

They are as follows:—

Four suits of ten, corresponding to the ten Sephiroth in the four worlds.

Four suits of court cards, kings, queens, knights and valets, corresponding to the letters of the name in the four worlds.

And in addition twenty-two trumps corresponding to the twenty-two letters of the Hebrew alphabet.

I should point out here that nearly all the games we play, such as chess, draughts and cards, are founded on mediaeval magical systems. And it seems more than probable that they were originally invented for the purposes of divination. Indeed one can look back to a period when drama originated from the ritual of the Mysteries and painting from the construction of talismanic images which should protect or avenge the owner, whether they were painted on his walls or carried in an amulet hanging from his neck-chain. Song was the sounding of mantrams, or evocatory ejaculations. Poetry was a spell made potent by its rhythms and metres. We have passed from this solemn world of superstition and eternal communion with supernatural beings, through the arts, into another world. We no longer believe in the consciousness of anything but ourselves. We answer our own puzzle as to the origin of consciousness by saying that in its early stages, it is irritability and chemical reaction. These are ugly words, and the thought is ugly. Perhaps we shall learn more about it if we wait a little while. We may find that Life is a beautiful creature after all, even when she is only fiery passion and shows herself in detonations and convulsions and in sudden flame and in sullen smoke.

The Kabbalistic system is the foundation of most of the *Theurgic* [or ceremonial magic] formulas that were practised in the Middle Ages. They are dangerous to the student because, although we are safe in endeavouring to attain to the Being of God, strange terrors beset us on every side the moment we try to understand the supernatural powers of the ministers of God. Iamblichus defends Theurgy on the ground that the Egyptian Hierophants practising it had themselves become supernatural beings. Theurgy may be said to be a right practice when the consciousness has been able to penetrate the consciousness of other species. A priest, limited to the experience of his own species, attempting to practise Theurgy for the small advantages of a special race, enters into the battle-field of nature with no equipment against disaster, and invites madness and misfortune, because that kind of smallness means a want of understanding of his own invulnerability or, I might call it, his own ultimate degree of being, which is the ultimate degree of the Being of Nature. The fool who is forbidden to use the practices of Theurgy is the fool who stands apart from life, himself an isolated spectator of its panorama; this is the ignorance which is death. Under the law, sin is folly and folly is sin, and the fool is battered and tortured until he learns wisdom. In order to try and grasp the idea

of the ultimate unity which is within us all now and here,
after the Kabbalistic fashion, let us use the symbol of the
mathematical point. Let us picture to ourselves all the
forms we know resolved into their last essence; that is, into
an infinite quantity of points of exactly similar appearance.
When we have called up this idea in our mind let us imagine
a consciousness in each of these points, but it must be
purely a consciousness of a self-sufficing nature, a feeling
of plenitude and well-being united to the certainty that
space only contains similar beings to itself and time can
produce no real change in its nature. This is called, I think,
by all mystics the consciousness of oneness, the solitude
which is the source of every change in time and space. The
centre is everywhere and the circumference nowhere.

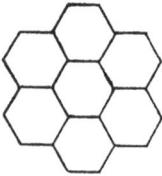

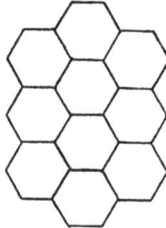

One surrounded by six.	Two surrounded by eight.	Three surrounded by nine.
THE GROUP OF SEVEN.	THE GROUP OF TEN.	THE GROUP OF TWELVE.

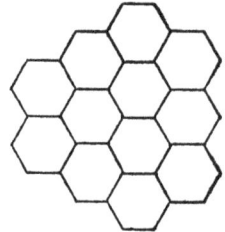

Let us again picture to ourselves the infinite number of
points arranged as a honeycomb so as to take up the most
compact relation possible. Now the idea of circumference
comes into existence. Magnified on the flat we see one
surrounded by a circle of six or three points surrounded
by a circle of nine or two by a circle of eight. (I will not
attempt to confuse matters by going into the relation of
solids; I am imagining a surface of points merely for the
sake of clearness.) We begin, therefore, with a relation of
one surrounded by six, two surrounded by eight, and three
surrounded by nine. We must now imagine a consciousness,

arising in the units, of a relation to other units. That is to say, interest or inquiry is awakened; the consciousness is no longer at peace in the assurance of its own omnipresence and plenitude; it becomes aware that it is in relation to other units. It is no longer all-sufficing, and the idea awakens in it that in addition to its own ineffable being there exist, potentially within it, innumerable powers of combination. Alone, it is surrounded by six possible relations. United to one other it is surrounded by eight potencies, or means of power. United to two others it is surrounded by nine potencies.

When this idea arises the point enters into relation with other points and becomes a line, a triangle, a cube and all the variety of created things, because its attention is transferred from the contemplation of the all-sufficing nature of pure consciousness to the contemplation of the endless variations of related consciousness. Consciousness of relation is the stirring of the Great Breath. The arising of intelligence from the intelligible substance does not change it any more than drops of water change when the waves pass through the ocean. The points are there unchangeably and eternally the same; but mutual relations arise, now here and now there, as the breath of life, or desire, passes from one to the other in curves or angles of different kinds. So it is with human consciousness, our attention is not fixed upon eternal substance until we search for it in the interior of our own sense of existence, but we are normally aware of consciousness as it relates us to our parts and to the history of our parts. We can even see it resembling the shadow coil of star dust we call a nebula or the embryo of a universe. We watch it churning and circling until the magic glamour makes us imagine that solid bodies come into existence as the whirling slows down.

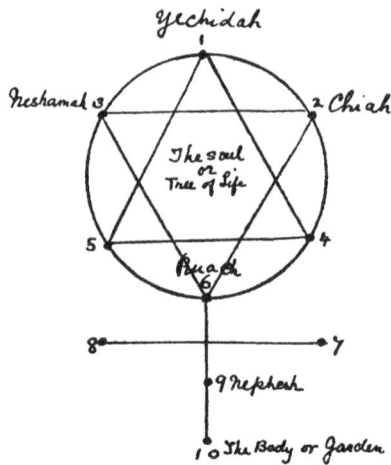

The Sephiroth and the parts of the Soul

To the Kabbalists the high part of the soul was in the state called *Yechidah*, isolation and unity, symbolized by the absolute consciousness of similar points. In the point itself this changes into the relative state called *Chiah*, or life, and the soul was life long before it entered into the cup of *Neschamah*, spoken of in the previous chapter. Neschamah means literally the Aspiring One, and this part of the soul passes between the unified absolute consciousness and the relative consciousness of life. It gazes first at one and then at the other, and its love creates *Ruach* [or Spirit], the Inspired One, the Son of the Mother, Neschamah. Finally *Nephesh*, meaning breath or spirit, is the name given by the Kabbalists to the automatic part of the soul which carries on the functions of life. These parts of the soul correspond to the numbers 1, 2, 3, 6, and 9, and are supposed to reach the body through the head, the heart and the powers of reproduction. It is interesting to compare the Hindoo belief that the four principal castes took their origin from the corresponding parts of the body of Brahma, the Creator.

We perceive, therefore, that the Kabbalistic Theurgists were well aware that two out of the five parts of the soul were on planes of consciousness in which the individual had no part. The link between these planes and the individual was the nature that aspires to life as a whole; that is to say, nature as the Centre which is everywhere. The two lower parts of the soul, Ruach and Nephesh, the inspired and the automatic, are of great interest; for Ruach, in its best sense, corresponded to the Messiah; it is complex, and is very nearly the same as the Antahkarana or interior creator, the image-maker of the Vedanta. It is the Egyptian *Ka* when it puts itself into the questioning attitude, before it becomes open to inspiration.

The Nephesh is reproductive, and repeats again and again the old ideas and the old circlings of the memory; but it is very important and can be taught to do almost anything by patient application. It appears to be incarnate memory; for it repeats what it has learnt, and appears to resent nothing except being required to give up old habits. It behaves like its prototype the number nine, which recurs eternally, and reduces all its multiples into the sum of itself. It is the force in us which clings to old paths, and explains new ideas by old platitudes.

Lastly in speaking of the Kabbalah as it has reached us we must remember that we have not received it from the Jews but from the Moors and the Italians and the Germans and the schoolmen of the Middle Ages. It is a cosmopolitan mixture of the ideas current in the fifteenth century, but it is far less interesting than other aspects of the same thought to which we will pass on.

Notes:
1. 'On the Kabbalah,' was originally printed in *The Occult Review*, Vol. VII: No. 4. London: William Rider & Son Ltd., April 1908. pp. 213-218.—D.K.
2. Florence Farr's Appendix of correspondences and the plate from Rosenroth's *Kabbalah Unveiled* was never printed in *The Occult Review's* serialization of her book.—D.K.

The Rosicrucians and Alchemists[1]

A legend arose in the time of the Lutheran outburst of a mysterious master called Christian Rosenkreutz, who was buried for a period of 120 years in the central cavern of the earth. His shrine was seven-sided, and all the symbols of the universe were said to have been found disposed round him in this place. The Egyptian tradition of Seker, the god in the central cavern of the *Duat*, evidently found an echo in the heart of the inventor of this legendary father of mysteries, and it will be interesting to try and discern the meanings of the main symbols of the Rosenkreutz legends in Egypt and in Germany.

The Egyptian *Duat*, or Underworld, was represented by a five-fold star, or star of five radiations, enlarging as they receded from the centre, and therefore not bearing the same symbolism as the pentagram. The Rose is fivefold in its structure and is a well-known symbol of silence. The stages of its existence pass from the bud, or potential state of pralaya, to the unfolding of its leaves as the pleroma, or fullness or manifestation of creative power. Consciousness, thought, reasoning, will, and the sense of individuality are five of its powers; the five senses are other manifestations of the same symbol. When the pollen of a flower is ripe the creative work begins, the petals fall and the fruit and seed are formed. The processes of life are a rhythmic coiling and uncoiling; a radiation and attraction, and an emanation or separation. The fruit coils round the seeds, the juices pass to and fro, and finally the husk of the fruit bursts and the seeds fall out separately as emanations, each complete in itself.

So in the degrees of human enlightenment the purest state is Being so unified and perfect that the kind of consciousness that depends upon comparison cannot exist. The second state is the sense of being without bounds, which is often called wisdom. The third state is discernment, or understanding, and may be attained by concentration of the subjective mind upon an object until full understanding is attained. And these states of the unmanifest consciousness are called *Sat-Chit-Ananda* in the Vedantic philosophy and *Ain-Soph-Aur* [Limitless Light] in the Kabbalistic philosophy; and *Ptah-Seker-Osiris* was the concrete image of these ideas in Egypt.

Now the Rose of the Rosicrucians was a more complicated symbol than the Cup. As we have seen the Cup was a symbol of creation, and its form was connected with the symbol of a circle in contrast to the Cross. The symbol of the Rose contains five petals and five divisions of the calyx. It is evidently the symbol of creation in activity, not in potentiality only. Perhaps we may believe the Rose to be a symbol of the subtle body of man, which is one with nature, and the Cross the symbol of the body and the name or word of man. The union of the Rose and Cross would symbolize a man able to unite himself to the great powers of Nature, or tatwas, familiar to us under their Hindoo names *Akasa* [Spirit], *Vayu* [Air], *Tejas* [Fire], *Apas* [Water] and *Prithivi* [Earth], or the kingdoms of sound, sensation, perception, absorption and reproduction more commonly called hearing, touching, seeing, eating and generating.

Now the notion of obtaining the natural powers of an adept is most apparent in the traditions that come through Egypt and Chaldea, and the idea of the super-essential state in contrast to power is most apparent in the Oriental traditions. The high caste Oriental has the aristocratic spirit that conceives the height of life on this world to consist in the delicacy of perception associated with perfect self-satisfaction, while the democratic spirit of the West cannot conceive itself without desires, struggles and potencies for gratifying desires; democracy wishes to do and to have; aristocracy is sufficient unto itself.

Rosicrucianism and Alchemy are both allegories constructed by these working democratic minds, and in the alchemical symbolism we can trace the exact degrees of initiation through which the man, still under the great race delusion of progress, must pass before he realizes that his real self is the same yesterday, to-day and for ever.

It is true in a sense that this treasure of all sages, this knowledge of Being which all mystics seek, forms itself vehicles in time and space in which it carries out the imaginations which spring from the relative side of absolute consciousness, and it is interesting to trace the different degrees of attainment.

Alchemical symbolism is mainly the symbolism of distillation. To take a simple process, let us imagine that we desire to obtain the white and the red tinctures from honey. The alchemist would put the honey in the cucurbite of an alembic. Placing it over a gentle heat he would drive the essential part of the spirit into the head or beak of the alembic, whence it would pass as steam into the neck of the receiver and become liquid once more as it cooled. This liquid was the white tincture, or spirit of honey mixed with water. This is the symbol of that concentration and meditation whereby the mind of man becomes subtilized and fit to perceive philosophical impressions. The white tincture is the symbol of light and wisdom.

But to obtain the red tincture of power a far more complicated process had to be performed. It consisted mainly of pouring back the distilled spirit upon the black dead-head that had been left as residue in the cucurbite and by the exercise of great care and the addition of certain matters acting upon the mixture in such a way that finally the whole of the original matter was distilled and no black dead-head remained and a wonderful red tincture was the result of the transmutation of the black nature.

This symbolical process involves the passing through definite stages of progress in the world of changing life. Let us imagine it carried out to its logical conclusion upon our own earth. We know that the mineral kingdom is the state in which form lasts for infinite ages and can stand great heat and cold without destruction. We know that the giants of the vegetable kingdom last many hundreds of years, but although the process of their growth and decay is prolonged they are not capable of resisting fire or of existing in the frozen zone. We know that certain animals, such as elephants, tortoises and parrots, live for very long periods of time. All these creatures have greater tenacity of existence in the forms or vehicles of life than the human creature.

It is also plain that as the earth becomes more and more subject to violent change, when the great floods and the ice and the burnings visit it, in its old age conscious life must exist in more enduring but less complex, sensitive, visible forms than it does at present. Now consciousness of Being is the name we give to the white tincture which the adept distils from his human form in the alembic of the mind. It is brought about by the fire of imagined emotion and devotion under the stress of intense concentration. To focus thought has the same effect as to focus sunlight. It becomes a force analogous to heat. It is, in a word, emotion evoked by the skill of the sage. In this fire the Adept raises his consciousness until it is separate from the gross body, and no longer aware of the objective world. Passing through the gate of dreams it enters the subjective world and lives in its own brightness. Here it learns that it can create infinite visions and glories, and here the saints rejoice, each in his own heaven. Here finally the sage perceives his own divinity and is united to his God. This is the white initiation in the eyes of the Rosicrucian doctors, and according to the scriptures of the alchemists the sage has gained the white tincture. The objective world only remains in his consciousness as blackness and ignorance and death. In his divine nature he seeks to redeem the dark world, to draw it up into the divine nature and make it perfect. His vision can now show him a world in which man can no longer exist in material human form. His own desire for wisdom has drawn up the human element out of the visible or objective state. He is no longer merely a man in a human body because his subtle body has possessed itself of the characteristic human faculty of self-conscious comparison, the origin of wit, laughter and criticism.

The humanity that is beyond animal consciousness has the power of acting and knowing at the same moment; it can seem one thing and know at the same time that it is another. It is not a noble quality; it is nothing more than the power of laughing at ourselves; and yet it is the great redeeming quality, for it is the germ of all wisdom and enlightenment.

The ordinary dreamer lives in his subtle body as the fool of his own fancy, and the dream shows how little human wisdom his subtle body has obtained; but the subtle body of an adept can perceive the illusionary formulation of panoramas of light and form arising from the half-seized impression of light falling at a certain angle across the red edge of a blanket and the linen of a sheet just as he closes his eyes. The dream of the sage is a consciously guided dream. Like an author, he writes his own dramas and delights in the joys and tragedies of his creations. He no longer suffers from the attacks and sorrows that his own mind creates, but observes them with excitement and interest. He watches his own tears and cuts into the heart of his own emotions.

These are some of the experiences of the sage who has transferred the human principle from the body of matter to the subtle body.

The material body may in this stage of enlightenment be considered as a beautiful and healthy animal; it carries on the physical functions in temperate ways, unaccompanied by the fantastic imaginations of a human being. And there is little doubt that the bull of *Apis* was considered to take the place of the body of the adept Osiris in this way. The body of a sacred animal would answer every purpose for the divine man whose invisible body had attained some degree of complex, conscious life. The nervous forces of the animal world act as the physical basis for the dream-powers of the subtilized or deified man.

In China the flying dragon, the mythical combination of all kinds of animal life, represents the body of the deified man that can command all the elemental states of matter that can exist in the air, the fire, the earth and the water. The dragon is the symbol of the material body of the being who has complete command of the elemental world and afterwards becomes the subtle body in the further stage of being of which we are told in Druid tradition.

When the earth grows older and complex animal forms such as flying-fish and sea-serpents and monstrous alligators, can no longer exist, another symbol must be taken from the writings of the Rosicrucian doctors and the alchemists, and we enter upon the study of the Tree of Life. He who eats of the fruit of the Tree of Life will become one with the Elohim, or creative gods, and will live for infinite ages.

Imagine the world enveloped in a great white cloud, moist and warm like a hot-house; giant palms and ferns and mosses dripping with moisture; a climate like that of the Cocoa-palm Islands off the west coast of Africa, where animals and men can only live a little time. In this world the adept would use some marvellous tree as the physical basis of his life; and his subtle body would have drawn up into itself all the forces of motion that make a tree less powerful to our minds than an animal. The subtle body in this state would have become a veritable dragon of complex forces. It would have drawn into itself the mixed sphinx-natures of the birds and the fish, the creeping things and the four-footed creatures. The dryad of each tree would be a mighty Druid; the great Pendragon would have his oak as a physical form and would exercise his powers in reality as we can imagine the ancient Druid sages exercised theirs in imagination.

This state of the subtle body may perhaps have been symbolized by the Green Dragon of the alchemists, but the Red Dragon arose after still further distillation.

Now we have to imagine a world all fire and molten glory of flame, in which no tree or flower could exist; a world in which wonderful agate trees would circle the white crystals of their pith with bands of violet and hyacinth and blue melting into stretches of pale chalcedony and shrouded in dark crystal bark, their branches glimmering with emerald leaves; a world in which mineral life has learned at last to show itself in perfect form, where light and fire glowed alternately and played with elemental shapes and images of beauty. And so, at last, we come to the last symbol of the alchemists—the symbol of the final perfection, the *Summum Bonum*, the Philosopher's Stone.

Let us imagine what that state would mean for the adept; his gross body a pure ruby, a perfect crystalline form with all the powers of growth, of nourishment, of reproduction drawn from the vegetable kingdom into his subtle body, carried on without disgust or satiety through the beautiful mediums of fiery blossoms and shining leaves; his subtle body almost visible as a light shining in the fiery world; his children flowers of flame and his physical form an everlasting memory of beauty; his mind an all-pervading consciousness in which blossoming imaginations arose or subsided under the law of his will; a perception unified with a faculty that ordered joy to succeed sorrow and sorrow to succeed joy because he knew that one cannot manifest without the other. A supreme artist, he would rejoice in creation; a supreme critic, he would rejoice in contrast.

So the red tincture would be attained and the black, the white and the red worlds explored and analysed in the imagination of the Rosicrucians and alchemists of the Middle Ages

We still see the same desire for progress among those who strive for the ancient stone here in this western democratic world of men who desire "to have" and "to do." But these circles of everlasting recurrence so dear to Friedrich Nietzsche are not what he called them. They are not aristocratic.

The aristocracy of mind is shown in the philosophy of Villiers de l'Isle Adam, who cried: "As for living, our servants can do that for us." It is the feeling of the great Buddhist intellect who sees that in the words "I am not" there is a wonder and a vision and song far exceeding the mere ideas of limited ecstasy and knowledge concealed in the words "I am."

Notes:

1. 'The Rosicrucians and Alchemists,' was originally printed in *The Occult Review*, Vol. VII: No. 5. London: William Rider & Son Ltd., May 1908. pp. 259-264.—D.K.

The Philosophy Called Vedanta[1]

IT will be seen from a system given in an Appendix[2] that the Vedantists as well as the Kabbalists have used the idea of analogy and correspondences. For the threefold nature of the Holy Spirit corresponds to the threefold nature of the gods and of humanity. And the fivefold permutation of the ultimate divine state corresponds to the fivefold permutations of nature in her dark or automatic condition and to the fivefold permutations of the subtle body of a man.

We find that the fivefold nature of the *Duat* of the Egyptians and the fivefold Rose of the Rosicrucians bear the same interpretations; and the fivefold mystery is related to the Trinity, because, besides containing the separated qualities of the Trinity as the blossom, the fruit and the seed-pod, it contains them, united as it were, as three branches on one tree, and it contains them in their earliest potential state in the likeness of the seed before it is grown to a tree.

These states which we have already studied under the Kabbalistic symbolism as the surrounding whirlings, the radiant centre, and the separated Sephiroth; and again as the three pillars of the Sephirotic Tree, and as the king, queen and knight of the Tarot cards, are called in the Vedantic system Sat, or Being; Chit, or Wisdom, the Divine Sophia; and Ananda or Ecstasy. The *Sat-Chit-Ananda* is also regarded as a unity which had arisen from a former potential or seed-like state.

The state of rest is sometimes said to consist of a whirling so rapid that coherent form or relation is impossible, exactly as in ecstasy the saint is so preoccupied with the wonder of his own spiritual exaltation that no exterior power can affect him sufficiently even for him to be aware of its existence. After rest these wheelings of the spiritual ecstasy gradually slow down and by a long series of convulsive movements and sounds of thunder Nature brings forth from form her passion and her dancing.

The story of the birth of tangible things seems to be common to the East and to the West. But the peoples of the East do not attach the same value to our present life as the peoples of the West are inclined naturally to do. They have kept the external life so simple that they are able to face death with a splendid courage. We have made it so complicated and acquired excellence in the arts and sciences with so much toil that we feel a regret at parting with the mechanism we have educated and disciplined. We fear that we shall by some accident or foolish ignorance find ourselves astray when we wander among the shades on the banks of the dark river.

We do not love the simple ecstasy of nature as they do. They love the gift that cannot be taken from them; we love the passing glories of this world of painful civilization. They do not believe progress is an eternal reality. The greatest of their philosophers have looked upon life as a farce to be acted with as much forbearance as possible. We cannot do this; it is impossible for an unphilosophic mind to attain this attitude. And who is there with a philosophic mind here? We all have a touching faith in the value of our own work and wisdom. So life in the East is seen to be an exquisite farce, and sometimes we have seen the dark mournful eyes of their princes watching our restless struggles and wondering that we should take so much trouble to disturb the world with our reforms. There is no object in living except to discover that living is a farce. What does it matter?

We can only mutter that these strange aloof beings who smile with sad eyes are mad. We are too much aware of our own worthiness. We deny that it is possible that the human race, and especially that part of it to which we belong, could have been created without a serious purpose; we fill life with serious purposes, and although we cannot do much for other people except give them mistaken advice, we still hope to find out something purposeful if we can only stay in the world long enough. I have said I have seen the sad eyes of a prince from the East wondering at the restless vulgarity of well-bred people. His face was of most wonderful perfection; and he said nothing, but moved about among the well-dressed rabble and went away quietly. Hours of instruction could not have taught me what the sight of that silent face stamped into my very soul: "I am here to learn to see through my own convictions. I am here to overcome the magician who has bewildered me. I am here to learn to know myself. That is the only purpose life has."

Another time I heard a certain Hindoo philosopher, said by the late Professor Max Müller to be very learned; and although he seemed to think abuse more effective than argument, his conversation was very interesting. He had evidently been talking about her religion to a benevolent English lady. When I came into the room she was saying:—

"There is something in all our hearts which makes us aspire to what is beyond."

The Hindoo.—That is all delusion and folly. You are ignorant of what man really is. You do not understand anything. These masters of religion you speak of are prophets whose work it is to enslave men. We, the teachers of the Highest come to free them from ignorance and delusion. We see down into the world of the prophets who bring religions into the world. No one can say, "I am the Son of God." God cannot be a father; that is a human relation. (Then in a thundering voice, he cried:) I am beyond all gods. I am Atman. This body is nothing; the only body I have is infinite ecstasy. (Ananda mayakosha.)

The Lady.—Yes, yes, that is all very well. But the God I speak of knows us and knows what we each require.

The Hindoo.—God does not know anything of the sort. His consciousness does not enter into the delusion of the foolish and ignorant. Oh, you are ignorant, you do not understand!

The Lady.—Oh yes, I do; more than you think. I want something higher than you teach. I want the Kingdom of God, not of man.

The Hindoo.—I tell you, you are ignorant. You do not know what man is; you must go to hell.

The Lady.—Oh, you believe in hell then?

The Hindoo.—Hell is being subject to delusions, and enjoying and suffering through the objects of delusion here. You win have to incarnate thousands and thousands of times.

The Lady.—But I don't want to.

The Hindoo.—You will have to. You don't want to die, but you will die, and your dying thoughts will carry you into some other body—man, woman, fish, bird.

The Lady.—I don't fear death.

The Hindoo.—Oh, you are ignorant; you cannot see that you are Infinite Spirit, all-pervading. I am That; you are That; she is That; he is That. There is no difference. That has no human relations; there is no father or mother or son about the matter.

The Lady.—I believe in a God.

The Hindoo.—Millions of your fellow-countrymen have got beyond that; they know these religions are fables and delusions.

The Lady.—Who died for me.

The Hindoo.—Martyrdom is a folly. It shows that a prophet does not know how to present his message. I should be a fool if I stood on the steps of your churches and said: "This is all wrong; pull down this place, this is all error." No, I speak to those who come to me for Truth. You had better go away.

After much persuasion she did go away. He was asked by some one else: "How did illusive power (Mâyâ) contain the five elements of which Brahma is devoid?"

He replied: "In the Eternal Omnipresent Existence of Brahma the following five forms are contained: (1) Omnipresence; (2) Potential Power; (3) Illusion in Potential Power; (4) Knowledge; (5) Bliss. As long as an Omnipresent Knowledge of the Three in One exists, that Knowledge is Brahma. But when in the same Brahma a little atom becomes separately conscious of the idea of Bliss, then that atom's knowledge became an active God and the knowledge of Bliss an illusive power of God (Mâyâ). The reflection of the knowledge of God in the Bliss became Jiva, or soul. It then forgot the knowledge of the Omnipresent Brahma and became an individual soul, and illusion was added to illusion and the five forms of Brahma emerged as the five elements we know. Salvation shall be for those who can recognize the reality underlying the illusive forms it dwells in."

This charming and naïve statement of an ardent believer in the Divine state possible to human beings interested me at the time, but I found the philosophy was attended by a simplicity of nature so complete that it was impossible to forget my own experiences sufficiently to become equally simple.

It is very difficult to accept Eastern teaching as to the acting of the life-farce, although one is quite willing to admit that, theoretically, life is a farce. Sometimes one imagines that the ideal guru is not a messenger from the East but a certain radiant state of consciousness symbolized as the root with three branches, or the Omnipresent Knowledge of the Three in One.

There is little doubt that the mind has a visible and an invisible workshop. Like a great smith it hammers out problems and questions. This gives us the sensation of thought. We set ourselves to think out the best way to attack such and such difficulties. We clamour at the gates of some barrier. Suddenly, without any opening of gates, without any trouble at all we are there, we know all about the subject and we wonder that we should have asked a question when we knew the answer all the time. It is just as if part of us would insist upon fixing its attention on the mechanism of our ears instead of listening to the sound flowing in. Our mind is an instrument which asks questions, but cannot answer them. It is the receiver of answers just as our ears are the receivers of sound. We have only to focus our attention, for the Knower is within and without; it is not an individual reflection of Atman, but it is the universal Atman; but we clothe it in numberless forms of gods and spirits, gurus and fetishes.

The Omnipresent Knowledge of the Three in One of the creative, subjective and objective states of the soul is a centre of radiance whence the three spring as illusionists, egoists and illusions, for egoism is the instrument of the illusionist. In the same way that the subjective mind is the instrument of the creative mind. The Omnipresent does not act in its state of union, but when separation takes place it appears as these phases of mind. Impulses bombard the personality and illusions are created because of the separated state of consciousness.

An hour ago a simple instance of the difference between the wise and the foolish way of trying to accomplish something happened to me. I had been searching a book of some five hundred pages for a half-remembered passage for about five minutes in vain. I gave up the struggle and named the part of the passage I wished to find. My hands turned the leaves idly for half a minute and then the first finger of my left hand pointed to the exact passage. No act of superstition on my part, no intervention of spirits or guides was necessary. I only expressed my desire clearly and without agitation. A great many times I have found this process of the mind succeed. The questioning attitude, like the prayerful attitude is efficacious. It is the right one both with myself and other people; it is the right way to work the mind. A clear statement of the need in words is necessary. To tighten up the muscles and to clench the teeth in making a physical effort do not produce so good an effect as the loosening of the muscles in order to let power rush through the body. The force that flows through the nerves is gathered in from all sides, and if the flow is uninterrupted by violent contractions there is practically no limit to it, and power and knowledge come to us easily. But although many people have received illumination when the mind assuming its radiant form discovered to them its power and touched its own root, the state of Omnipresent Consciousness, they will not believe that so mighty a power can in reality attune itself to their petty human spirits. Like the English lady who talked of her God with confidence, they create illusive ideas for themselves and worship Omnipresent Consciousness as something outside and beyond them. To persist in this want of faith in unity involves a fall deeper and deeper into delusion and separation, as the lady was warned by the philosopher, whose words she could not understand.

The root of the delusion of progress is in this want of faith. We can all ask questions now; we need not wait for some indefinite future. Ask the question and listen to the answer which comes in the form of an idea without apparent process of thought or logic. It is true that after the idea has come, the logical faculty delights to play with it and examine its perfections. For logic is always useful as a means of convincing ourselves that what we have made up our minds to do is right. Logic is the plaything of the mind and slowly goes over the ground that the radiant Mind traversed in the millionth of a second.

When a few people meet together and ask trivial questions while they tilt a table, they succeed in getting answers because the least common measure of their minds is capable of answering foolish questions foolishly. If their purpose and questions are on more important matters the least common measure may be of a higher quality. But it is very seldom that two or more can think out high problems better than one in solitude after concentration and meditation; for these practises are the best means for stilling thought and hearing wisdom.

It is possible that a guru and his chela [or pupil], whose natures are specially attuned to each other, may produce thought and expressions of thought impossible to either of them alone, especially when the two are filled with devotion. For the questions of one stimulate the higher mind of the other. The guru can answer any intelligent question put to him, and the oracles of the ancient world were examples of this very common power; for it is an almost universal experience with teachers of all sorts that they can often give extraordinarily clear replies on subjects they had not considered beforehand when an intelligent pupil asks them a sufficiently definite question.

Socrates stimulated himself by the questions he asked, and it is a strange thing that the method is not more freely used in the elementary discipline of the mind practised by all who seek to know themselves. There is an interchange between all who ask and all who answer as subtle as the interchange between an orator and his audience. He gives them words; they give him life; and each quickened pulse desiring light feeds his eloquence with a more brilliant inspiration.

Notes:

1. 'The Philosophy Called Vedanta,' was originally printed in *The Occult Review*, Vol. VII: No. 6. London: William Rider & Son Ltd., June 1908. pp. 333-338.—D.K.

2. Florence Farr's Appendix of correspondences was never printed in *The Occult Review's* serialization of her book.—D.K.

The Tetrad, or The Structure of the Mind[1]

THE real man, otherwise the mind, whether it is the average mind deep in its own little groove or the supermind in touch with its race, has for characteristic, a power of passing from one state to another. The mind is a great actor, and the meanest intelligence is capable of recognizing that it can see all questions from many different points of view. To take a very obvious instance, a man respects the emotion of love when he feels it himself, but he professes the profoundest contempt for any other man who loves the same woman. He is therefore capable of seeing this passion at once as an ennobling and a degrading state; and he is able to compare the two points of view. He sees it from the centre and he praises it. He sees it from the outside and he pours contempt upon it. In the same way the mental perceptions can look at all questions, from these two points of view, at least. The mental power of passing from the centre to the circumference is analogous to the mental power of attaining absolute consciousness when the mind is stilled and returning to relative consciousness when the mind is in motion.

I have already pointed out that we must consider the symbol of the absolute to be a mathematical point, and the symbol of the intelligence to be a triangle, or tetrad; because the intelligence deals with the relation between points, and not with the points themselves. This form of the tetrad, or a pyramid of three equilateral triangles, is the symbolic root of relative existence, or, in other words, nature. It contains four points and twelve possible relations, because each point stands in three possible relations to each other point.

To understand this clearly it may be useful for a student to construct a magnified tetrad of points for himself with four marbles piled in a pyramidal form. We have taken the point itself as absolute consciousness; its relation with other points as relative consciousness; but its relations with one other point is said to manifest not as creation but as wisdom, an enlightening sympathy barren but resplendent, the aim of all philosophers. It is the relation of two perfectly wise beings rejoicing in perfection together.

Why does this inward and outward consciousness fall into the fatal act of creation? The answer of most traditions is "Because wisdom is also symbolically a serpent, and tempts to experiment." "Compare" is the fatal cry of the dual conscious mind; that is to say, the mind that can view itself from the interior or the exterior point of view. It has developed a power, and it wishes to use it. "Let me compare," it says. Then the third point, the power of criticism arises, and we have the subjective, objective and the spirit of comparison, which three form the fourth point, an opinion, or conviction. Each tetrad of consciousness is founded on its own particular conviction; and when we speak of fulfilling the law of our own being, we mean we must carry out our root conviction to its logical conclusion, and see it through all possible manifestations.

Mind, then, is the manifestation of what we call our identity or root conviction. This great Father in the Beyond takes on one form or another, but its insatiable will to experience and to compare devours all the endeavours of the little beings we, in an unenlightened state, call ourselves. The Father mind is the germ of relative consciousness arising as a phenomenon in dual consciousness, and all manifestations arise from it and its power of fixing the attention on certain patterns in the whole and rejecting others. In essential nature we are the infinite substance consisting of similar points, but we chose to limit our consciousness to the relation between certain parts of the whole, and to weave a pattern in the Cosmos. The great Father mind, or source of minds, is symbolized by the four lettered name of God [or Tetragrammaton] by the Rabbis, as the Divine Tetractys or Chatur-Vyaha by the Brahmins, and with the little mind within each of us. We are all engaged in weaving smaller patterns that we may compare and judge of our experiences when we are drawn back into the fountain of being.

This happens every day. Each meditation is a Judgment Day, each dream is a heaven or a hell, just as we have penetrated or not into the peace which passes understanding and comparison. In the *Bhagavat Purana* we find the mental faculties divided into four parts, making five phases in all, because the idea of the whole is added to the idea of the separated four parts. In Sanscrit the whole is called Antahkarana, really equivalent to the imagination, or image-maker, the creative power of the mind. The parts are called manas, buddhi, chitta and ahankara. Ahankara is the egoity of the image-maker, buddhi is the bias of the image-maker, chitta is the will of the image-maker, and manas the doubts and comparisons of the image-maker. The doctrine of the Vedanta is that egoity is the root of all delusions, because it deludes us into believing the temporal to be eternal and the eternal to be the temporal. The little self arranged or designed by the image, or pattern-maker, takes upon itself the character of the unchangeableness of the points of eternal consciousness.

One aspect of the mind is the Logos, or famous four-lettered Name of many systems of symbology; the *Dad*, or Word of the Egyptians. Para, or the first aspect, is manifested in breath or Prana, ☉ [Sun]; Pasyanti, the second, in the mind, ☽ [Moon]; Madhyama, the third, in the powers of the mind; Vaikhari, the fourth, in articulate expression. These are analogous to the Rabbi's four methods of interpreting

Scripture, through its rhythm, its melody, its phonetics and the literal meaning of the myths and fables used as methods of instruction. To paraphrase the *Emerald* Tablet, we may say that meditation on the word proceeds from the Sun-Father, or Prana, the Moon-Mother, or mind; the ten winds, or currents, carry it in their bosoms, and it is nourished by the earth, or physical sound of the name.

Close thought on the nature of the mind is a necessary part of the discipline of the mystic, for the mind is the bridge between the absolute and relative consciousness; it invites objective appearances to their invisible source through the subjective world.

In the *Bhagavat Purana* we read of the word that: "The Para division is said to be the latent sound, and is seated peacefully on the Serpent of Eternity as equilibrated will." The Pasyanti is the cause, or germ-thought, the Serpent that can dissolve all illusion and can cause all delusions; it is egoity. The Madhyama is friction making sparks. Sometimes it is the desire for complexity, or related consciousness, and sometimes the desire to return to simplicity, or absolute consciousness. It understands truly and falsely and is memory, doubt and sleep, buddhi, or judgment. Vaikhara is speech, and like melted butter can feed flame, as thought can feed desire.

The secret power of the word or mind sits as Vasudeva upon the Serpent and creation arises from him. The story is as follows (*Bhagavat Purana*, scanda 3, chapter viii.):—

"When this universe was submerged in the waters of rest, the eyes of Vasudeva remained closed in sleep. He opened his eyes and saw himself lying on the Serpent King. He delighted in himself, remaining passive. Within him were all dreams and beings in latent being; only the power of time was manifest. Vasudeva dwelt as fire in wood with all his powers controlled, excepting only Time; having slept thus for 1,000 Yuga cycles, he found the lotuses of his body and the thread which unites them. That thread was pierced by Time and threw out energy, and, small as it was, it grew from his navel, and by the action of Time, which awakens law of cause and effect, it suddenly grew and became a lotus flower. Brahma was in that and looked on all sides (space came into being) and became four-faced, and he searched everywhere confused, and cried: 'Whence am I? Whence this lotus?' And he searched in vain. Then in his ignorance he began the work of creation."

Here we see the story of the mind of man, which despairs of discovering its own origin and creates images because it has no true wisdom. It cannot reduce itself to the dual state, which is omniscient, nor to the state of unity, which is Supreme until it has gained the power of comparison from experience.

We pass on to the Serpent mind which creates as egoity a world of images, the fuel of thought; then to the more familiar world of logical judgment, and finally to the world of speech where thought is expressed and manifested, as fire is made manifest in flame.

The Vedantic method of studying the nature of the tetrad as a symbol of the imagination, or mental power, is well described by Deussen in *The Religion and Philosophy of India*. (English translation published by T. & T. Clark, 38, George St., Edinburgh, 1906.)

"When using the mind, senses and physical organs, a man believes his impressions of external objects of sense to be real (waking life); when only using the mind, apart from waking impressions, a man believes memories of these impressions to be real (dream); when the mind also rests, all consciousness of particular objects ceases and the man exists subjectively without conscious convictions of any kind (dreamless sleep); when the mind is gathered up by the consciousness and contrasted with all subjects and objects as undifferentiated substance it is set free from existing things and is in the state called liberation."

Now waking and dreaming are both states of delusion. In waking life we reflect a manifold universe which has the same origin as ourselves. The perceptions of the waking life are obliterated in dream, and the perceptions of the dream life are obliterated on waking. We feel ourselves in bonds to both these conditions. We are surprised by what is done and said by others and by ourselves. We cannot control anything, because we are in bondage to our belief in the objective reality of these states.

There are two ways of dreaming. In the first the breath-father remains in its place and fashions a new world of forms from the material collected in its waking hours. In the other the breath-father forsakes the body and moves whither it will and sometimes finds difficulty in returning; it is said that the spirit wanders up and down in the garden of the body.

Of the state of deep sleep it is said: "Just as there in space a hawk or eagle folds its weary wings and drops to the ground after its circling flight, so the spirit hastens to the state where it knows no desire nor sees any dream-image, where the life breath is in union with thought."

But the yogi discovers a fourth state called Turiya. While awake and perfectly conscious he stills his mind as if in a brown study and commands it to go where he chooses, to cogitate on any problem he chooses, and to enlighten him on any subject he chooses, to build up for him the dream he prefers and to carry out his commands as a faithful servant instead of commanding him as a cruel tyrant.

The Western psychologist confesses his inability to compete with a yogi in the exercise of these faculties, which can be developed by an intelligent culture of the imagination. The Eastern writers (until Deussen arose to interpret them) have written in such obscure language that it is difficult for a Western mind to grasp that the mighty achievement they call "stilling the mind" has been familiar to us all in our childhood.

Who among us has not, on being suddenly offered "a penny for his thoughts," found his mind to have been a complete blank or else an ecstatic fairy vision far removed from the understanding of his mortal companions?

The invariable reply is "I was thinking of nothing," or "My thoughts were far away."

Of course if we sit down and say, "Now I will make my mind a blank," the mere act of wondering whether we have made the mind a blank prevents us from success, and it is here that the use of symbol comes as a boon to the struggling student of his own soul. Take the tetrad, the solid three-sided pyramid based on an equilateral triangle, and say: "I will meditate on this symbol of the fire-mind, I will think of the fire which melts thought into a molten mass and of the smith who hammers out forms." The mind, clinging to the symbol of its own primitive nature, the image whence sprang all imaginings, will hold fast to the meditation; it will next see itself in crystalline forms branching from the mineral into the vegetable symbolism; then in motion becoming animal in its nature and gradually, through comprehension of its own nature, becoming man as he will be when this object is accomplished. We are here in order that through experience we should learn to know ourselves. When we have accomplished this perhaps our minds may become mighty ghosts using the bodies of animals for our lower needs; or still more powerful and immortal as we learn that our bodies need never move, and that by the power of our imaginations all experiences are within us. I have already hinted that in those days when the world grows old and nothing but great forests can subsist, we, being part of the consciousness of earth, must accomplish a power that can act through the forms of life then possible. By degrees, as we melt once more into a cloud of fiery dust, the fire mind which has learned to understand the true nature of the crystalline life, that has followed its form back to the ultimate symbol of mind, can still retain its consciousness; for that symbol signifies the Eternal Relation eternally potential in the Eternal Absolute.

In this suggestion we see the idea behind the symbolism of the Tree of Life and the Philosophers' Stone. We in our natural state are so proud of belonging to the human species that we refuse to see what wonderful possibilities lie outside that form of life. But as I have already said in chapter iv, the ancient Egyptians realized the possibility of their divine ancestor, Osiris, manifesting through the form of a bull. The sacred animals of Egypt were provided with every means of leading a perfectly healthy physical life. Let us suppose a great mind exists in a ghostly body, but to impress its will upon the physical world it needs a dedicated vehicle, such as the body of an animal. The great mind, acting through the physical life of the purified animal, can function in a more manifest way than is possible to a mind bereft of all physical apparatus. The freshly killed animal offered before the *Ka* statue of a great ancestor, not so much as a sacrifice, but as a means of manifestation, was another form of this idea. Now we all expect a time to come when human life cannot be supported on this earth. It may become once more a land of dragons and amphibians. These creatures may develop a nervous system that can respond to and interpret consciousness even more rapidly than the human nervous system.

The idea that the simpler the form the truer the medium is not a new one. Mathematical truth is the only truth we can rely upon; crystalline form may be a far more subtle medium for revelation than organic form. The mysterious organ of the brain, which mystics say is the organ developed only by the highest of the human race, contains little sand-like crystallizations. Tree dryads may possibly be all the more active because their bodies are immovable, just as a yogi tells us that when his body is still as the dead his knowledge is clearest and his bliss is the most ecstatic.

The essential mind and the Stone of the Philosophers are the same, and its simplest form is the tetrad. The method of studying the mind by forcing the imagination to take certain forms is perhaps one of the most practical forms of mind-training that has ever been invented. It is especially useful to us in helping us to realize that we can dominate and alter form by application of the attention. Infinite possibilities of relative consciousness lie all around us, and through the use of mathematical symbols we can use and develop these elemental states of consciousness to the uttermost. We can combine them in infinite complications, and as long as we do not forget our own essential state we shall not be lost in the illusions of this world, or in the delusions of the madhouse.

Notes:
1. 'The Tetrad, or The Structure of the Mind,' was originally printed in *The Occult Review*, Vol. VIII: No. 1. London: William Rider & Son Ltd., July 1908. pp. 34-40.—D.K.

On the Play of the Image-Maker[1]

THE Latin word *ludo*, I play or sport, is the root forming all such words as ludicrous, illusion, delusion, and so on. In Sanscrit the corresponding word is *lîla*, and it is used to describe the work of creation.

We learn then, that it is the special work of the creative part of the mind to create delusive forms. I do not think we sufficiently realize that our life is in reality a series of illusions, and how much what we call our characteristics depend upon the bent of our illusions. For instance, if we accept the delusion that we are healthy we overcome disease; if we are more open to the delusion that we are unhealthy, we give way before disease. This individual susceptibility to notions and impulses is the really interesting thing in the study of a human being. It does not arise from birthright and country. If it did twins would be identical. The theory of rebirth in numberless human forms does not explain the mystery, but only makes it more remote. The conscious mind has not much to do with it, nobody would consciously prefer to be in pain. The practical way of controlling it appears quite absurd; for it is not, as is sometimes asserted will-power, but a kind of hypocritical pretence of believing what reason tells us is untrue. The assumption of an attitude of faith and the assertion of belief in words has over and over again been found to concentrate the unknown illusionary powers, and bring about some wished-for event.

This is one of the great puzzles of life. I remember years and years ago I was asked to regulate the beating of a hypnotized person's heart by saying aloud, "Your heart is to beat slower—a little quicker—that is right." I merely said the words without any assumed faith. I did not believe, I only said the words, and to my greatest astonishment the heart beat exactly as I told it to beat.

Effort, as commonly understood, has no effect comparable to this calm imperative statement. If a thing is really desired it cannot be attained, because real desire contracts and blocks up the passage of the words with emotion, or in some other unknown way. The law appears to be: There is nothing in the world you cannot do as long as you do not care whether it is done or not.

We have all seen this on the stage. We have seen one actor struggle and sweat over his part, and we have admired his devotion and intelligence. We have seen another peacefully expressing himself and the whole audience hanging on his words. The hard worker is generally getting £10 a week and the other £100.

Evidently calmness is a great power and desire a great weakness. A kind of mathematical precision is part of the expression of power; and I believe the faith in symbolic magic arises from the mathematical precision of symbols, because the contemplation of a perfect symbol gives perfect form to the imagination.

Let us consider the analogy between the imagination and the Demiurgos, or creator of the world. Because the symbol of the earth is imperfect it is said the creatures arising from it are liable to imperfection. The sphere of the earth is said to be flattened at the poles, and through some such bias in its form its laws and cycles are imperfect and vary unaccountably. The malformation is its individuality or personal character; and it is necessary to us to try and discover the laws of its lawlessness. They interest us.

In an old Sanscrit story the immortal bird sits with the mortal on the phantasmal Tree of Life, and the immortal does not eat of the fruits, but lives in contemplation. The mortal bird eats of the fruits, and they are joy and sorrow, life and death. A Vedic hymn tells how Death sits carousing with the gods at the foot of this tree, and the mortal who eats of the fruits is under the dominion of Death, who is the lord of the gods.

Why does the immortal Spirit sit twin-like beside the mortal and watch him live and die and fill himself with desire and satiety? It interests him. The link between the mortal and immortal brothers is so close, so terribly close, that throughout the life of the mortal the immortal feels unwillingness at the thought of separation.

I have heard people in the flush of health say that they do not care for the mortal side, and they would throw away their bodies as if they were old clothes. It would mean no more to them. It is an interesting mood. But only a mood. All mystics know that it is easy for an expert to enter the state of rigid trance voluntarily and to attain to a state of temporary death, in which the heart appears to stop beating. He may repeatedly and gladly leave his body but is he willing gladly to let his body leave him? I do not believe it.

I think the reason of this secret feeling of resentment against death is that the immortal bird has a certain satisfaction in watching his mortal brother, and the deep root of the sorrow of death and decay is this immortal regret. The mortal life is a drama set up for the pleasure of the immortal witness; it often takes so deep an interest that tears fall from immortal eyes and cause wonders to appear on earth. The more miserable the story of the life the more exciting the drama becomes, and the less willing the immortal spectator is to say, "Enough." For that is all that is necessary to put an end to sorrow and decay and death and sin.

Why do we sit out these sordid dramas? Why does not our eternal consciousness retire from the contemplation of disease and cruelty? Can it be because it is tired of contemplation of eternal beatitude and perfection?

The oldest traditions say that is why.

Let us consider the question through our own feelings. When we first study philosophy, when we first open our eyes upon the world as baby children, we ask, "Why is everything happening?" Later on we say, "Why, if Unity is perfect, does creation arise from it?" The wise teacher replies, "You yourself came out from perfection; you separated yourself as a drop from the ocean, as a spark from the fire. Why did you do so?"

We wonder for a little, and then we remember it was because perfection and silence and unutterable bliss cannot be endured continuously; and so the immortal bird watches the sorrows of his mortal brother.

The absolute watches the relative, and it is his sport and play to do so.

So long as we consider ourselves as separate from this creator, the notion of being the sport of the gods is intolerable; and no human being in that stage of belief will hear of it with patience.

But when we have faced the appalling truth that we have ourselves constructed all that we know and remember because we chose to do so, we end by excusing ourselves. We know that we love in our hearts a rhythmical existence; we are willing to pass into trance, to attain consciousness of unconsciousness. We want to remember or forget at will, and let all the universe of suns and stars disappear in a flash. We want to be able to return; we do not want to be forced to return. We want to attain liberation and pass from the plenitude of the absolute into the deprivation of the relative without losing consciousness in the transitional states.

Again, there is a kind of drunken pleasure in this very loss of consciousness, and in sharing the delusions of the exterior world. We feel the inebriation of romance when we read about the "new knowledge" and the inevitable periods of elemental substances, of the shapely groupings of quivering particles. There is a triumph in the thought that little mortals have constructed means of measuring space and reckoning periods. But what does it matter really when we sleep or die what laws may govern the exterior world?

The only knowledge that could make a real difference to us would be the knowledge of how to enter into the consciousness that underlies these ultimate aggregations, these fiery dances of that primal state in which spirit and matter can no longer be distinguished from each other. The only thing of eternal importance is that we should be released from the notion that the particular groupings that we call our minds and bodies are the only groupings that make consciousness possible. We want to be able to understand and enter into the consciousness of simple organisms, of simple elements, and finally into the consciousness of universal life and its actions, desires and being.

How does any human soul attain this beatitude? Not because it can float in the ethers of the seven heavens, but because it has entered into the consciousness of further degrees in the scale of that simplification which ends in the knowledge of simplicity and wholeness united. The soul rests in the field of some larger knowledge than that represented by the ministers of visible nature.

We believe that the consciousness of organic life is diffused everywhere in temperate regions, and the *Dionysian* ecstasy of that consciousness comes to all who seek it faithfully in communion with organic life. The colder and more remote ecstasy of *Apollo* is that of the still more diffused consciousness of inorganic life. It is more ordered and less immediately destructive, although the passions of intense fiery energy blast the forms of organic life and fling them into a limbo of unconscious deprivation. For each degree of the mysteries must be attained slowly by delving into the last secrets of Being. How clear consciousness must be in those Apollonian regions of inorganic being, unclogged by the slow motions of cells and the life they imprison! It can dart from sun to sun, seeing without eyes to blind it, hearing without the ears which deafen it to all but a little range of sounds. But before the ecstasy of *Eros* even the ecstasies of Apollo pass away, and in the blank etherial spaces the shining creators flit in the radiance that they themselves shed. All these ecstasies have been experienced by mystics who have described them over and over again. We need not wait till the whole world is fire and dew to know Dionysos and Apollo and Eros; they are all of them within reach of our hands, for they are the names we have given to states of the imagination and that which is beyond the making of images.

When we can attenuate our consciousness to the degree in which we can discern the substance of the stars, it is with us here. When we achieve this division or subdivision and realize that we can have a continuous consciousness woven through and through all degrees of substance, from the white life of the hottest star to the frozen death of the blackest moon, something is gained, and if the dream of existence is only a dream at least it will be free from the fears which make us sacrifice the noble aims of life to the ignoble means of living. And if there is no other life than this we are living now, to give a greater dream to others is better than to destroy and humiliate them in order that we may give alms to them and treat them with condescension. We cannot be great in the way of the world unless there are others who are small; we cannot be loved unless others are despised; we cannot earn unless others starve. But if our minds are great, then we shed a great blessing, for we no longer want anything which is limited; we do not want anything which others want, for we are satisfied by what we are in our own consciousness and do not need the possession and desires of the rest.

When we see this clearly we partake dimly in the play of the gods. We build up forms and watch them fade away. We initiate ideas which gradually start into life and fly on their own wings, and all the time we rest on the sure basis of the Gnosis which tells us form and sound will pass continuously into other forms and sounds, but the eternal Watcher remains. He is the immortal bird that does not eat of the tree of delusive life, but sits in its branches and sees them pass and fade and grow again in ever-varying form. He is God, and He is man when man has learnt to know who he is.

Notes:
1. 'On the Play of the Image-Maker,' was originally printed in *The Occult Review*, Vol. VIII: No. 2. London: William Rider & Son Ltd., August 1908. pp. 87-91.–D.K.

The Tree of Life[1]

Much that is interesting, and much that is incomprehensible, has been written about the *Tree of Life*, and there are many aspects that it is impossible to touch on in so short a space, but I hope to put before my readers a few practical suggestions with regard to its mysteries.

I must, however, in order to make my meaning clearer, deal shortly with the nature of trees, before approaching the myths and symbolism of the Tree of Life.

Now the nature of a tree is in all essentials the exact reverse of the nature of an animal. It is quite possible to imagine substance in such an exceedingly primitive state that the only sensation it enjoyed was attraction or repulsion. A secondary state then evidently arose in which substance was separated into vegetable stuff, which plunged its head into the earth, and animal stuff which reared its head into the air. If we think for a moment of the general structure and functions of animals and vegetables we shall see that the root and branches of a tree correspond to the head and limbs of an animal, and are placed relatively in opposite directions. An animal is more inclined to make an art of the way it devours its food; while the vegetable devotes its whole faculty for making life beautiful to the reproduction of itself and its kind, and conversely we find the neighbourhood of the earth in both cases is productive of useful rather than ornamental results.

One is perhaps apt to be a little bitter against the average cocksure opinion that the biped animal is the finest thing that Nature has achieved. We look out of our windows at the tall, silent trees which stand unmoved for hundreds of years, making no sign of what we call intelligent life, and in our pride because we can move, because we can speak and so endeavour to conceal our unpleasing thoughts, because of our railways, our commerce and our wars, because of our capacity for abasing our minds before the superstitions created by our imaginations, because of the necessities of our existence which are so shameful Schopenhauer has wondered how we dare face each other; because of all these things we stand self-crowned as the Kings of Creation. Are we so sure that we are really in a higher, holier state than the patient watchers who uncomplainingly permit us to cut them down and hack them in pieces in order that we may build ourselves dwelling places in which to cover up our shame?

That we have a great spiritual destiny I believe, but I do not believe that our animal form will remain for ever the most satisfactory vehicle in which our spirits can press forward in their search for The Great Peace. I can even imagine that in some other world, under more favourable conditions, the Vegetable kingdom has attained to that perfection or immaculate state in which the Spirit of Life and Wisdom can be received. Camille Flammarion, the French astronomer, has described his visions of distant planets in which this inversion of life, as we know it, has taken place, and it is not difficult to conceive that in such a world bees and ants, although here they have constructed the most elaborate social systems we know, may there be the mere ministrants of the holy Dryads and wise beings who manifest themselves in the form of trees. The Tree Spirit would rest in the Temple Nature had constructed for it, absorbed in the idea of the beauty that is beyond form, while the winged creatures would come and go among the flowers in faithful worship of the highest.

Plants were the first form of organic life in our world, for without them life of any other sort is impossible. All living matter is manufactured by plants under the influence of sunlight out of material floating in the air, and animals can only exist by eating what the plants have laid by for their own use. This is a very important point and cannot be sufficiently realised in treating of The Tree of Life. Plants are, in fact, the only things that know how to make living material from inorganic substance.

Before dealing directly with the myths of The Tree of Life, I will quote some passages from Mr. J.F. Hewitt's interesting book on the *Ruling Races of Prehistoric Times*, (1894). He says:—

"In India that we find the village of the aboriginal tribes invariably arranged so that the Sacred Grove (*Sarna*), in which the trees of the primitive forest are still left standing, is the central point of the place. It is here that we find the explanation of the reverence for the tree, the parent-tree of all the early races of India. ... The earliest villages were those founded by the Dravidian races who called themselves sons of the tree. ... They made the village, and not the family, their national unit, and made it a rule ... that the mothers and the fathers of the children born in their village should never belong to the same village, and that the children should be brought up by their mothers and maternal uncles without the intervention of their father, and should be regarded as the children of the Sacred Grove in which they were born. These tree worshipping people were the ancestors of the Amazons of Asia Minor, of the Basques and of the agriculturalists of the Neolithic age."

"The village makers of the early Stone Age carved their villages out of forests, just as their successors now do, by stripping the trees of their bark with their stone celts and burning the timber when dried. The holy shrine or grove, dedicated to the Gods of Life, was cut off from the unproductive forest, the abode of demons and malicious ghosts, by the cultivated land which surrounded it, which represented the encircling and guarding snake. Under the shade of the grove (*sarna*) the maidens of the village danced the seasonal dances with the young men of a neighbouring township, and in this way the birth of children was made possible. The children were called the sons and daughters of the Mother Tree and the Saturnalia celebrating the union of their parents were looked upon by the statesmen of Matriarchal times as a safeguard of the national welfare. The children were brought up by their maternal uncles who taught them their duties as members of the tribe and village. It was the influence of the Matriarchal tribes who reproduced everywhere the Holy Groves consecrated to the gods of Greece, Rome, Palestine, and Asia Minor, together with the worship of the Dryads or spirits of the woods. It was their influence which sanctified the Mother Tree, the Tree of Life, the palm tree of Babylonia, the sycamore or fig-mulberry of Egypt, the fig tree of the Biblical story of the fall of man, the olive tree of Greece, the pine or Christmas tree of Germany, and the Tree which is still planted on the top of every house built in South Germany."

"Mâyâ, the mother of Buddha, went to the sacred grove when her son was to be born, and sought the protection of the tree god by grasping the sacred Sal-Tree (*Shorea robusta*) while her son was brought forth. The same incident is reproduced in the story of the birth of Apollo at Delos."[2]

These interesting details lead us naturally to the inquiry into the ancient Myths regarding the Tree of Life. In the first book of the Vedas, Hymn cxxxv., the earth is called the Island of the Tree Yambu. Siva is the Lord of the Yambu Tree that grows in the centre of the plateau which crowns Mount Meru. It yields the Soma drink of immortality to the gods. Its roots are in the world of Death, its shadow is on the moon. It reaches to the Heaven of the Gods and its trunk is the sustaining axis of the universe. It sprung from Amurnam when churned by the gods in the heaven of Indra. Yama, the god of the Shades, sits at its feet.

The Soma juice, or Elixir of Life of the Hindu, answers exactly to the Haoma of the Persians. Su and Hu were the

Gods of wisdom and power in Egypt, while the words Su, Hu and Khu all imply shining spirit of life. Another Hindu tradition has been handed down to us that the name of the head of all initiated hierachies is the Ever-Living-Human-Banyan-Tree.

The ancient inhabitants of Chaldea, now commonly called Akkadians, possessed a hymn which sings of a dense pine tree growing in a holy place. Its fruits of brilliant crystal extend through the liquid abyss. Its place is the central spot of the earth, its foliage is a couch for the Spirit of Peace, Zicum. In the heart of this holy tree, which casts a shade like a forest that no man has entered, dwells the great mother who is over the heavens; and in the midst is *Damu-zi*, the son of life. At the vernal Equinox a pine tree was cut so that the sap of life flowed from it, and the image of *Damu-zi* was hung on it, and the whole carried into the sanctuary of the mother of the gods, adorned with woollen ribbons and spring violets.

(To be concluded.)[3]

Florence Emery
London, England.

Notes:
1. 'The Tree of Life,' was originally printed in *The Lamp*, Vol. IV: No. 7. Toronto, Canada: Privately printed, 15 September 1900. pp. 194-197.—D.K.
2. Please note that these quotes are not an exact quote from Hewitt's book.—D.K.
3. This article was never concluded because *The Lamp* ceased to exist after the publication of the 15 September 1900 issue.—D.K.

The Magical Literati

of Florence Farr

HATSHEPSU, accompanied by her KA,
making perfume offerings.
(From the Temple of Dêr el Bahri.)

The Magical Literati

of Florence Farr

2012
GOLDEN DAWN RESEARCH TRUST

The Magical Literati of Florence Farr was first published in this edition by The Golden Dawn Research Trust in 2012.

The cover page illustration 'The Rose Cross' is from Israel Regardie's *The Complete Golden Dawn System of Magic*, 1984.

Contents

Flying Roll No. II:
Purity and Will

(November 24th, 1892.)

PART I - A SECOND SUBJECT FOR CONTEMPLATION
By G.H. Frater N.O.M.[1]

BEFORE even Strength of Will, you must have Purity of Body, Mind, Intellect, and of Emotion, if you hope for magical power. The Spiritual Powers will flourish only as you starve the animal Soul, and the animal soul is largely dependent on the state and treatment of the animal body. The animal man is to be cared for and protected, kept in health and strength, but not petted.

Be moderate in all things human. Extreme ascetic habits, are to you here, a source of another danger, they may lead only to a contemplation of your own Heroism, in being abstinent. To be truly ascetic is indeed to submit to discipline and to curb unruly emotions, thoughts and actions. But, who is a slave to his animal Soul, will practice vice in a Forest; while he who restrains himself among the crowds of a city, and passes through a busy life—unpolluted, shows more resistance and suffers severer discipline, and shall obtain greater reward.

PART II - REMARKS UPON THIS SUBJECT FOR CONTEMPLATION
By V.H. Frater L.O.[2]

Spiritual Power results from the *transmutation* of the gross animal nature. The various centres of sensation in the human body can be harmonised by the equipose or circulation in the contrary forces of attraction and repulsion—or, on the other hand, the vehicle of excess.

If "Our God is superlative in His Unity", analogy must follow between the greater and lesser worlds. One of Danton's clairvoyants once described a lake of gold in the centre of the earth, and we have the injunction "Visita Interiora Terrae Rectificando Invenies Occultum Lapidem."[3] The primum mobile of even a commonplace vessel is placed in the centre of the ship. Now, the place of power and seat of equipoise is in numbers; the number 5 as has been pointed out:—

1 2 3 4 5 6 7 8 9.

That is the Sephirah Geburah "Where there is Gold", whose lineal figures traced with the single point uppermost is the most powerful continuous symbol there is.

By the sign of the Microcosm is the symbolized the athanor of the Alchemist—at everybody's hand with out their knowing it. "A strong and decided will", says Levi, "can in short space of time arrive at absolute independence".

The condition of equipoise is therefore necessary before the manipulation of the Will is even possible; and Will is something more than the ascending of our higher desires over the lower, being a kind of electric force, the executive of desire. In this light it is the creative power, which fashions according to the ideal form or subsisting types. It is therefore through the agency of the will that the hidden becomes manifest, whether in the Universe or Man.

The student has to learn to arouse those forces within him or her self. This masterly indifference is the great theme of the *Bhagavada Gita* and the Indian Yogis—in fact both East and West unite in teaching us to preserve that equal mean between two extremes, which is the law of immortality.

Part III - Three Suggestions on Will Power
By V.H. Soror S.S.D.D.[4]

Head 1. In studying the nature of the will force we are aided by our Minutum Mundi scheme. Mars, Geburah, Fire, Aries, each expressive of the will force on different planes, are all red in colour. The Red Lion was used as a symbol by the Alchemists to express the highest powers of the Adept. The whiteness of purity having been attained, the heat must be violently increased, until by the redness of perfection strength manifests itself.

Head 2. Now the danger which attends out labours arises from attempting to exercise this will power, before we have purged ourselves of ignorance and darkness. Until we know we must refrain from doing. This sounds as if the case was pretty hopeless; but we have each in our own persons all the materials for experiment, and as long as we desire light, and do all we know to obtain it, we are not likely to do ourselves permanent harm; but at the same time we cannot be too careful in applying the very superficial magical knowledge we have at present to others, especially to those who are uninitiated. The danger I have found is that though the first step is most difficult, I mean it is extremely difficult to gain control over another's will so as to alter their natural tendencies; yet this is done the force you have set in motion becomes almost uncontrollable, the other individual seems sometimes to only live in your presence, and the last state of that person is worse than the first. This is a noticeable feature in the cases of those who have been cured by faith healers; or professional hypnotists.

Head 3. Having explained these dangers, the method I advise for cultivation of will is, to imagine your head as centre of attraction with thoughts like rays radiating out in a vast globe. To want or desire a thing is the first step in the exercise of Will; get a distinct image of the thing you desire placed, as it were, in your heart, concentrate all your wandering rays of thought upon this image until you feel it to be one glowing scarlet ball of compacted force. Then project this concentrated force on the subject you wish to affect.

Notes:
1. G.H. Frater N[om] O[mnis] M[oriar] was W. Wynn Westcott's 7°=4° motto..–D.K.
2. V.H. Fra Levavi Oculos was the Second Order motto or Percy Bullock.–D.K.
3. "Visita Interiora Terrae Rectificando Invenies Occultum Lapidem" translates as "Visit the Interior of the Earth and by Rectification Thou Shalt Discover the Hidden Stone".–D.K.
4. V.H. Soror S[apientia] S[apienti] D[ona] D[ata] was the Second Order motto for Florence Farr.–D.K.

Flying Roll No. IV:
An Example of Mode of Attaining to Spirit Vision and What was seen by Two Adepti.

By V.H. Sorores S.S.D.D., and Fidelis, 5°=6°. [1]
(November 10th, 1892.)

Secure for an hour or for longer absolute freedom from interruption. Then alone, or with one or two other Adepti, enter the vault, or private chamber. Remain in silence and contemplation for several minutes.

Rise, and perform the Kabbalistic Cross and prayer. Then proceed to contemplation of some object, say a Tarot Trump: either by placing it before you and gazing at it, until you seem to see into it; or by placing it against your forehead or elsewhere, and then keeping the eyes closed; in this case you should have given previous study to the Card, as to its symbolism, coloring, analogies, *etc.*

In either case you should then deeply sink into the abstract ideal of the card; being in entire indifference to your surroundings. If the mind wanders to anything disconnected with the card, no beginner will succeed in seeing anything spiritually.

Consider all the symbolism of the Tarot Card, then all that is implied by its letters, number, and situation, and the paths connected therewith.

The vision may begin by the concentration passing into a state of reverie; or with a distinct sense of change, something allied in sensation to a faint, with a feeling urging you to resist, but if you are highly inspired, fear not, do not resist, let yourself go; and then the vision may pass over you.

If you have anything occur or disturb you, you will come to readily enough—or as from a doze; otherwise the vision ends of itself, or some can check it by will, at any stage, others can not, at first, at any rate.

Example

The Tarot Trump, the Empress was taken; placed before the persons and contemplated upon, spiritualized, heightened in coloring, purified in design and idealized.

In vibratory manner pronounced Daleth. Then, in spirit, saw a greenish blue distant landscape, suggestive of the mediaeval tapestry. Effort to ascend was then made; rising on the planes seemed to pass up through clouds and then appeared a pale green landscape and in its midst a gothic temple of ghostly outlines marked with light. Approached it and found the temple gained in definiteness and was concrete, and seemed a solid structure. Giving the signs of Netzach Grade (because of venus) was able to enter; giving portal signs and 5°=6° signs in thought form. Opposite the entrance perceived a cross with three bars and a dove upon it; and beside this, were steps leading forwards into the dark, by a dark passage. Here was met a beautiful green dragon, who moved aside, meaning no harm, and the spirit vision passed on. Turning a corner and still passing on in the dark emerged from the darkness on to a marble terrace brilliantly white, and a garden beyond, with flowers, whose foliage was of a delicate green kind and the leaves seemed to have a white velvety surface beneath. Here, there appeared a woman of heroic proportions, clothed in green with a jewelled girdle, crown of stars on her head, in her hand a sceptre of gold, having at one apex a lustrously white closed lotus flower, in he left hand an orb bearing a cross.[2]

She smiled proudly, and as the human spirit sought her name, replied:

"I am the mighty Mother Isis; most powerful of all the worlds, I am she who fights not, but is always victorious, I am that Sleeping Beauty who men have sought, for all time; and the paths which lead to my castle are beset with dangers and illusions. Such as fail to find me sleep;—or may ever rush after the Fata Morgana leading astray all who feel that illusory influence—I am lifted up on high and do draw men unto me, I am the world's desire, but few there be who find me. When my secret is told, it is the secret of the holy grail." Asking to learn it, [she] replied:—

"Come with me, but first clothe in white garments, put on your insignia, and with bared feet follow where I shall lead."

Arriving at length as a Marble Wall, pressed a secret spring, and entered a small compartment, where the spirit seemed to ascend through a dense vapor, and emerged upon a turret of a building. Perceived some object in the midst of the place, but was forbidden to look at it until permission was accorded. Stretched out the arms and bowed the head to the Sun which was rising a golden orb in the East. Then turning, knelt with face towards the center, and being permitted to raise the eyes beheld a cup with a heart and the sun shining upon these; there seemed a clear ruby colored fluid in the cup. Then Lady Venus said: "This love, I have plucked out of my heart and have given it to the world; that is my strength. Love is the mother of the Man—God, giving the Quintessence of her life to save mankind from destruction, and to show forth the path to life eternal.

Love is the mother of the Christ—Spirit, and the Christ is the highest love—Christ is the Heart of Love, the heart of the Great Mother Isis—The Isis of Nature. He is the expression of her power—She is the Holy Grail, and He is the life blood of spirit, that is found in this cup."

After this, being told that man's hope lay in following her example, we solemnly gave our hearts to the keeping of the Grail; then, instead of feeling death, as our human imagination led us to expect, we felt an influx of the highest courage and power, for our own hearts were to be henceforth in touch with hers—the strongest force in all the world.

So then we went away, feeling glad that we had learned that "He who gives away his life, will gain it." For that love which is power is given unto him,—who hath given away his all for the good of others.

Notes:
1. S.S.D.D. was the motto of Florence Farr, and F[idelis] was Elaine Simpson.—D.K.
2. She also had a shield with a dove upon it.—N.O.M.

Flying Roll No. VI:
A Note upon Flying Roll No. II

By G.H. Frater D.D.C.F., 7°=4°[1]

WITH regard to the admirable note by V. H. Soror S.S.D.D. on
Will Power and Use—I would suggest that: Before bringing the
scarlet ray into such intense action in the Heart, as is explained
by her, that the Adept should elevate his thought and idea to the
contemplation of the Divine Light in Kether, and considering
Kether as the crown of the head, to endeavour to bring a ray
from thence, into his heart—his Tiphareth through his path of
Gimel and then to send the scarlet ray into action; the effect will
be powerful and the process safer: otherwise there is a risk to the
heart, and a risk of fever, if it be frequently done.

Notes:
1. "G.H. Frater D.D.C.F." was the Golden Dawn Motto of S.L.
   MacGregor Mathers who was one of the founding members
   of the Golden Dawn. Mathers full Motto was *Deo Duce Comite
   Ferro* which translated as "With God as my leader and the
   Sword as my companion".—D.K.

Flying Roll No. XIII:
Secrecy and Hermetic Love

By V.H. Soror S.S.D.D.[1]

WE have all no doubt heard of the terrible physical tests applied in Egyptian Initiations and are aware that violence amounting to torture was used in the Ancient Mysteries before the Neophyte was considered fit to take the first steps in his Ascent of the Mountain of God.

Though the methods of our Order are different the Spirit is the same, and unless we have learned indifference to physical suffering, and have become conscious of a Strong Will, a will which fears nothing fate can do to us, we can never receive a real Initiation.

These ceremonies in the lower grades of Our Order are principally active in disciplining our minds; they lead us to analyse and understand ourselves. They deal with the Four states of Matter, the Four Elements of the Ancients which with their synthesis answer to the five Senses. Our Senses are the paths through which our Consciousness approaches the central power which for want of a more accurate word I will call the Will.

It is the object of our lives as initiates to bring this Will to such a state of perfection, strength, and wisdom, that instead of being the plaything of fate and finding our calculations entirely upset by trivial material circumstances, we build within ourselves a fortress of strength to which we can retire in time of need.

The natural Man is a chaotic mass of contradictory forces.

In the higher grades of the First Order, (by presenting a perfectly balanced series of symbols to the senses) we endeavour to impress upon the imagination of the initiates, the forms under which they can obtain perfection and work in harmony with the world force.

In the 0°=0° Ceremony the principles most insisted on are Secrecy and Brotherly Love. Apart entirely from the practical necessity for secrecy in our Order, it is the fact that Silence is in itself a tremendous aid in the search for Occult powers. In darkness and stillness the Archetypal forms are conceived and the forces of nature germinated. If we study the effects of calm concentration we shall find that in silence, thoughts which are above human consciousness clothe themselves with symbolism and present things to our imagination, which cannot be told in words.

The more thought and concentration of purpose that precedes an action, the more effective and effectual it will be. Again in talking on subjects such as these, there is always a terrible danger of personal influence or obsession coming into action. The Eagle does not learn to fly from the domestic fowl "nor does the Lion use his strength like the horse", and although knowledge is to be gained from every available source the Opinion of others should receive the very smallest attention from the true student of Life.

Free yourselves from your environments. Believe nothing without weighing and considering it for yourselves; what is true for one of us, may be utterly false for another. The God who will judge you at the day of reckoning is the God who is within you now; the man or woman who would lead you this way or that, will not be there then to take the responsibility off your shoulders.

"The old beauty is no longer beautiful; the new truth is no longer true," is the eternal cry of a developing and really vitalised life. Our civilisation has passed through the First Empire of pagan sensualism; and the Second Empire of mistaken sacrifice, of giving up our own consciousness, our own power of judging, our own independence, our own courage. And the Third Empire is awaiting those of us who can see—that not only in Olympus, not only nailed to the Cross, but in ourselves is God. For such of us, the bridge between flesh and spirit is built; for such among us hold the Keys of life and death.

In this connection I may mention that the 0°=0° of the Grade of Neophyte has a deep significance as a symbol; a o means nothing to the world—to the initiate in the form of a circle it means all, and the aspiration of the Neophyte should be "In myself I am nothing, in Thee I am all; Oh bring me to that self, which is in Thee".

Having so far considered some of the thoughts that the practice of silence may bring you let us proceed to the subject of brotherly love.

We must of course take the word, as we take all higher teaching, as a symbol, and translate it for ourselves into a higher plane.—Let me begin by saying that any love for a person as an individual is by no means a Hermetic virtue; it simply means that the personalities are harmonious; we are born under certain influences, and with certain attractions and repulsions, and, just like the notes in the musical scale some of us agree, some disagree. We cannot overcome these likes and dislikes; even if we could, it would not be advisable to do so. If in Nature, a plant were to persist in growing in soil unsuited to it, neither the plant nor the soil would be benefited. The plant would dwindle, and probably die, the soil would be impoverished to no good end.

Therefore brotherly love does not imply seeking, or remaining in the society of those to whom we have an involuntary natural repulsion. But it does mean this, that we should learn to look at people's actions from their point of view, that we should sympathise with and make allowances for their temptations. I would then define Hermetic or Brotherly

Love as the capacity of understanding another's motives and sympathising with his weaknesses, and remember—that it is generally the unhappy who sin.

A crime, a falsehood, a meanness often springs from a vague terror of our fellows. We distrust them and ourselves.

It is the down-trodden and the weak whom we have to fear; and it is by offering them sympathy and doing what we can to give them courage, that we can overcome evil.

But in practising Hermetic Love, above all things conquer that terrible sting of love—jealousy. The jealousy of the benefactor, the jealousy of the lover, or the friend, are alike hateful and degrading passions. Jealousy is deeply rooted in human nature nourished by custom, even elevated to a virtue under the pretence of fidelity.

To see human nature at its very worst you have only to listen to the ravings and threats of a person who considers his monopoly of some other person's affection is infringed. This kind of maniacal passion is the outcome of the egotism á deux, which has been so fostered by romance.

But it is natural to wish to help and be necessary to those we love, and when we find others just as necessary or helpful, to feel bitterly that our "occupation" is gone; but these regrets will be impossible to us when we can live in the world realising from day to day more fully that the highest and best principle within us is the Divine Light which surrounds us, and which, in a more or less manifested condition, is also in others. The vehicle may be disagreeable to us, the personality of another may be antipathetic, but latent light is there all the same, and it is that which makes us all brothers. Each individual must arrive at the consciousness of Light in his own way; and all we can do for each other is to point out that the straight and narrow path is within each of us. No man flies too high with his own wings; but if we try to force another to attempt more than his strength warrants, his inevitable fall will lie at our door.

This is our duty towards our neighbours; our duty towards God, is our duty towards ourselves; for God is identical with our highest genius and is manifested in a strong, wise, will freed from the rule of blind instinct.

> He is the Voice of Silence,
> The Preparer of the Pathway,
> The Rescuer unto the Light.

Notes:
1. S.S.D.D. was the motto of Florence Farr.—D.K.

The Lecture on the Pillars

By V.H. Frater S.R.M.D.[1]

In the explanation of the Symbols of the Grade of Neophyte, your attention has been directed to the general mystical meaning of the Two pillars called in the Ritual the "Pillars of Hermes" of "Seth" and of "Solomon." In the 9th chapter of the *Ritual of the Dead* they are referred to as the "Pillars of Shu," the "Pillars of the Gods of Dawning Light," and also as "the North and Southern Columns of the Gate of the Hall of Truth." In the 125th Chapter, they are represented by the sacred gateway, the door to which the aspirant is brought when he has completed the negative confession. The archaic pictures on the one Pillar are painted in black upon a white ground, and those on the other in white upon a black ground, in order to express the interchange and reconciliation of opposing forces and the eternal balance of light and darkness which gives force to visible nature.

The black cubical bases represent darkness and matter wherein the spirit, the *Ruach Elohim*, began to formulate the Ineffable Name, that Name which the ancient Rabbis have said "rushes through the universe," that Name before which the Darkness rolls back the birth of time.

The flaming red triangular capitals which crown the summit of the Pillars represent the Triune manifestation of the Spirit of Life, the Three Mothers of the *Sepher Yetzirah*, the Three Alchemical Principles of Nature, the Sulphur, the Mercury and the Salt.

Each Pillar is surmounted by its own light-bearer veiled from the material world.

At the base of both Pillars rise the Lotus flowers, symbols of regeneration and metempsychosis. The archaic illustrations are taken from the vignettes of the 17th and 125th chapter of the *Ritual of the Dead the Egyptian Book of the Per-em-Hru or the Book of Coming Forth into the Day*, the oldest book in the world as yet discovered. The Recension of the Priests of Oɴ is to be found in the walls of the Pyramids of the Kings of the 5th and 6th Dynasties at Sakarah, the recensions of the 11th and 12th Dynasties on the sarcophagi of that period, and the Theban recension of the 18th Dynasty and onward is found on papyri, both plain and illuminated. No satisfactory translation of these books is available, none having been yet attempted by a scholar having the qualifications of mystic as well as Egyptologist.

The *Ritual of the Dead*, generally speaking, is a collection of hymns and prayers in the form of a series of ceremonial Rituals to enable the man to unite himself with Osiris the Redeemer. After this union he is no longer called the man, but Osiris with whom he is now symbolically identified. "That they also may be One of us," said the Christ of the New Testament. "I am Osiris" said the purified and justified man, his soul luminous and washed from sin in the immortal and uncreated light, united to Osiris, and thereby justified, and the son of God; purified by suffering, strengthened by opposition, regenerate through self-sacrifice. Such is the subject of the great Egyptian Ritual.

The 17th Chapter of the Theban recension consists of a very ancient text with several commentaries, also extremely old, and some prayers, none of which come into the scheme of the original text. It has, together with the 12th chapter, been very carefully translated for the purpose of this lecture by the V.H. Frater M.W.T.,[2] and the V.H. Soror S.S.D.D.[3] has made many valuable suggestions with regard to the interpretation. The Title and Preface of the 17th Chapter reads:

"Concerning the exaltation of the Glorified Ones, of Coming and Going forth in the Divine Domain, of the Genies of the Beautiful land of Amentet. Of coming forth in the light of Day in any form desired, of Hearing the Forces of Nature by being enshrined as a living Bᴀɪ."

And the rubric is:

"The united with Osiris shall recite it when he has entered the Harbour. May glorious things be done thereby upon earth. May all the words of the Adept be fulfilled."

Owing to the complex use of symbols, the ritual translation of the Chapter can only be understood by perpetual reference to the ancient Egyptian commentaries, and therefore the following paraphrase has been put together to convey to modern minds as nearly as possible the ideas conceived by the old Egyptians in this glorious triumphal song of the Soul of Man made one with Osiris, the Redeemer.

"I am Tum made One with all things.

I have become Nu. I am Ra in his rising ruling by right of his power I am the Great God self-begotten, even Nu, who pronounced His Names, and thus the Circle of Gods was created.

I am Yesterday and know Tomorrow. I can never more be overcome. I know the secret of Osiris, whose being is perpetually revered of Ra. I have finished the work which was planned at the Beginning. I am the spirit made manifest, and armed with two vast eagle's plumes. Isis and Nephthys are their names, made One with Osiris.

I claim my inheritance. My sins have been uprooted and my passions overcome. I am Pure White. I dwell in Time. I live through Eternity, when Initiates make offering to the Everlasting Gods. I have passed along the Pathway. I know the Northern and the Southern Pillars, the two Columns at the Gateway of the Hall of Truth.

Stretch unto me your hands, O ye Dwellers in the centre. For I am transformed into a God in your midst. Made One with Osiris, I have filled the eye socket in the day of the morning when Good and Evil fought together.

I have lifted up the cloud-veil in the Sky of the Storm. Till I saw Ra born again from out of the Great waters. His strength is my strength and my strength is his strength. Homage to you, Lords of Truth, chiefs of Osiris rules. Granting release from Sin, Followers of Ma where rest is Glorious. Whose throne Anubis built in the day when Osiris said:

Lo! A man wins his way to Amentet. I come before you, to drive away my faults. As ye did to the Seven Glorious Ones who follow their Lord Osiris. I am that Spirit of Earth and Sun.

Between the Two Pillars of Flame. I am Ra when he fought beneath the Ashad Tree, destroying the enemies of the Ancient of Days. I am the Dweller in the Egg. I am he who turns in the disc. I shine forth from the horizon as the gold from the mine. I float through the Pillars of Shu in the ether. Without a peer among the Gods. The Breath of my mouth is as a flame. I light upon the Earth with my glory. Eye cannot gaze on my daring beams as they reach through the Heavens and lick up the Nile with tongues of flame. I am strong upon Earth with the strength of Ra. I have come into Harbour as Osiris made perfect. Let priestly offerings be made to me as one in the train of the ancient of Days. I brood as the Divine Spirit. I move in the firmness of my Strength. I undulate as the Waves that vibrate through Eternity. Osiris has been claimed with acclamation, and ordained to rule among the Gods. Enthroned in the Domain of Horus where the Spirit and Body are united in the presence of the Ancient of Days. Blotted out are the sins of his body in passion. He has passed the Eternal Gate, and has received the New Year Feast with Incense, at the marriage of Earth with Heaven.

Tum has built his Bridal Chamber. Rururet has founded his shrine. The procession is completed. Horus has purified, Set has consecrated, Shu made one with Osiris, has entered his heritage.

As Tum he has entered the Kingdom to completed union with the Invisible. Thy Bride, O Osiris, is Isis, who mourned thee when she found thee slain. In Isis, thou art born again. From Nephthys is thy nourishment. They cleansed thee in thy Heavenly Birth. Youth waits upon thee, ardour is ready at thy hand. And their arms shall uphold thee for millions of years. Initiates surround Thee and Thine enemies are cast down. The Powers of Darkness are destroyed. The Companions of Thy Joys are with Thee. Thy Victories in the Battle await their reward in the Pillar. The Forces of Nature obey Thee. Thy Power is exceeding great. The Gods curse him that curseth Thee. Thine Aspirations are fulfilled. Thou art Mistress of Splendour. They are destroyed who barred the way."

The 125ᵗʰ Chapter is concerned with the entry of an Initiate into the Hall of the Two Columns of Justice, and commenced with a most beautiful and symbolic description of Death, as a journey from the barren wilderness of Earth, to the Glorious Land which lies beyond. The literal translation of the opening lines is as follows:

"I have come from afar to look upon thy beauties. My hands salute Thy Name of Justice. I have come from afar, where the Acacia Tree grew not. Where the tree thick with leaves is not born. Where there com not beams from herb or grass. I have entered the Place of Mystery. I have communed with Set. Sleep came upon me, I was rapped therein, bowing down before the hidden things. I was ushered into the House of Osiris. I saw the marvels that were there. The Princes of the Gates in their Glory."

The illustrations in this chapter represent the Hall of Truth as seen through the open leaves of its door. The Hall is presided over by a God who holds his right hand over the cage of a hawk, and his left over the food of eternity. On each side of the God is a cornice crowned by a row of alternate feathers and Uraei symbolizing justice and firey power. The door leaf which completes the right hand of a stall is called "Posessor of Truth controlling the Feet," while that on the left is "Possessor of strength, binding the male and female animals." The 42 Judges of the Dead are represented as seated in a long row, and each of them has to be named, and the Sin over which he presided has been denied.

This chapter describes the introduction of the initiate into the Hall of Truth by ANUBIS, who, having questioned the aspirant, receives from him an account of his initiation, and is satisfied by his right to enter. He States that he has been taken into the ante-chamber of the Temple and there stripped and blind-folded, he had to grope for the entrance of the Hall, and having found it he was reclothed and anointed in the presence of the Initiated. He is then asked for the Pass-words and demands that his Soul should be weighed in the Great Balance of the Hall of Truth, whereupon ANUBIS again interrogates him concerning the symbolism of the door of the Hall, and his answers being found correct, ANUBIS says: "Pass on, thou knowest it."

Among other things the initiate states that he has been purified four times, the same number of times that the Neophyte is purified and consecrated in the ceremony of the Neophyte. He then makes the long Negative Confession, stating to each Judge in turn that he is innocent of that form of Sin over which he judges. Then he invokes the Judges to do him justice, and afterwards describes how he had washed in the washing place of the South, and rested in the North, in the place called "Son of the Deliverers" and he becomes the Dweller under the Olive Tree of Peace, and how he was given a tall flame of fire and a sceptre of cloud, and made a lake of it. The initiate is then brought to the actual Pillars, and has to name them and their parts under the symbol of the Scales of Balance. He also has to name the Guardian of the Gateway who prevents his passage, and when all these are propitiated, the plea of the Hall itself cries out against his steps, saying "Because I am silent, because I am pure," and it must know that his aspirations are pure enough hand high enough for him to be allowed to tread upon it. He is then allowed to announce to THOTH that he is clean from all evil, and has overcome the influence of the planets, and THOTH says to him: "Who is He whose Pylons are of Flame, whose walls of Living Uraei, and the flames of whose House are streams of Water?" and the Initiate replies "OSIRIS!"

And it is immediately proclaimed:

"The meat shall be from the Infinite, and thy drink from the Infinite. Thou art able to go forth to the sepulchral feasts on earth, for thou hast overcome."

Thus, these two chapters, which are represented by their illustrations upon the Pillars, represent the advance and purification of the Soul and its union with Osiris, the Redeemer, in the Golden Dawn of the Infinite Light, in which the Soul is transfigured, knows all, and can do all, for it is made One with the Eternal God.

KHABS AM PEKHT
KONX OM PAX
LIGHT IN EXTENSION!

Notes:
1. V.H. Frater S.R.M.D. was the Second Order motto for S.L. Mathers.—D.K.
2. V.H. Frater M.W.T. was the Second Order motto for M.W. Blackden.—D.K.
3. V.H. Soror S.S.D.D. was the motto of Florence Farr.—D.K.

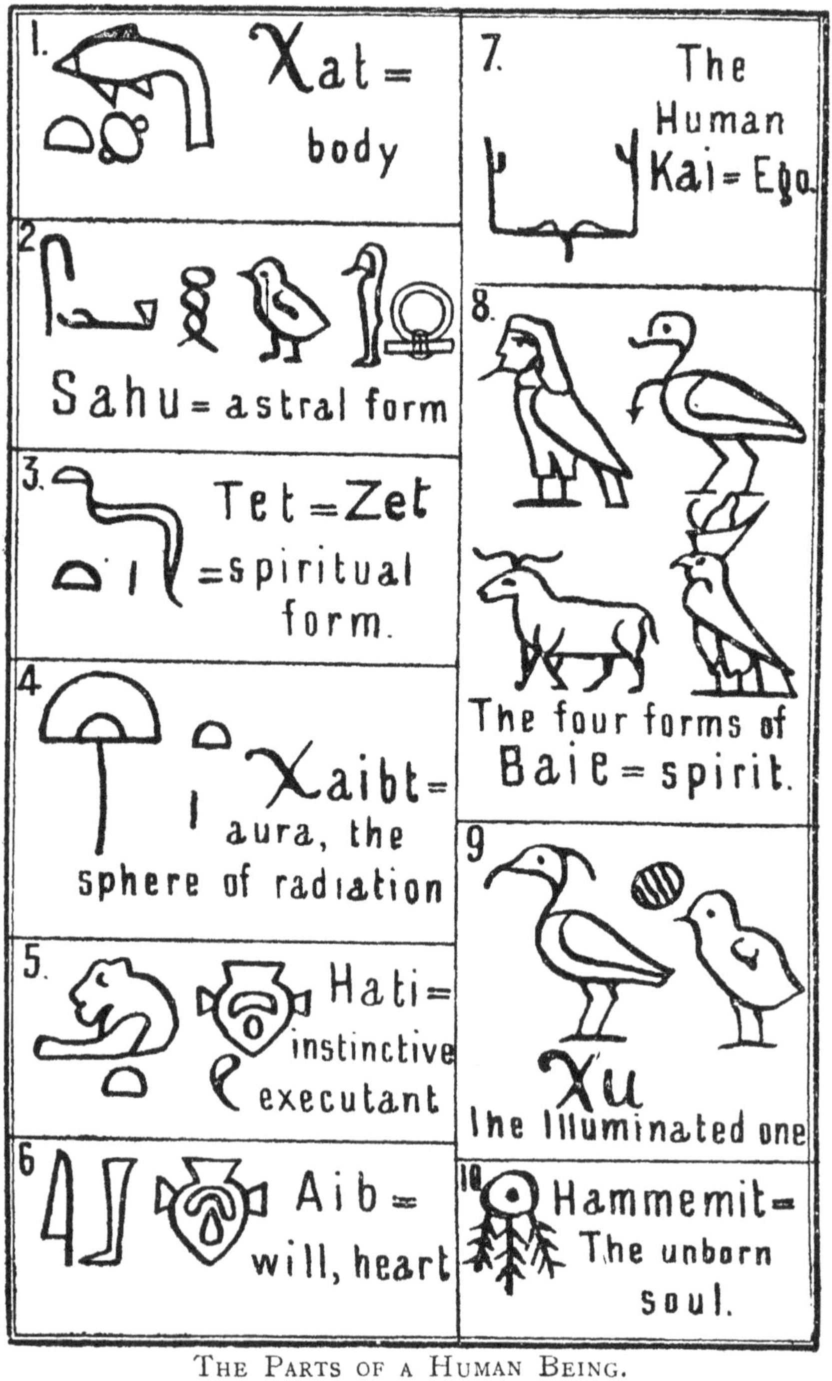

THE PARTS OF A HUMAN BEING.

THE PARTS OF A HUMAN BEING.

Determinative.	Egyptian Name.	Equivalent in English.
A Fish	= Khat or Kat	- Body, Corpse.
A Mummy and a Seal	= Sahu	- Elemental Body, Astral Body.
An Upright Snake	= Tet or Zet	- Spiritual Body, Soul.
A Fan	= Khaibt	Radiations of the Sahu; the Sphere or Aura, Emanation, Odour, etc.
The Forepart of a Lion	= Hati	Executant, Human heredity, Habit, Instinct.
A Vessel with Ears as Handles	= Aib or Ab	The Will, similar to the animal Will, but containing within it the germs of the Spirit and Human Ego, in the form of an Egg and a concave receptacle.
The Upraised Hands	= Kai or Ka	- The Individuality, the Human Ego.
A Hawk, Heron or Ram	= Ba or Baie	The penetrating Mind, the link with the Divine.
The Bennu Bird	= KhouKhu, or Yekh	The Magical powers. The Shining one. The Augoeides of Greek philosophy.
The Radiating Sun	= Hammemit	The Unborn Soul; apparently a separate emanation of the Solar Light.

Egyptian Magic.[1]

By V.H. Soror S.S.D.D.

THE study of Magic, which has now fallen into disrepute was, among the Egyptians, regarded with a veneration hardly accorded to the highest Philosophy in modern times.

To the Ancient Egyptians the most eminent man was he who had by hard training gained supremacy over the Elements, from which his own body and the Manifested World were alike formed; one whose Will had risen Phœnix-like from the ashes of his desires; one whose Intuition, cleansed from the stains of material illusion, was a clear mirror in which he could perceive the Past, the Present and the Future.

The Kings and Priests of Egypt were the elect of those who had studied with success in the "School of Wisdom," a Philosophical Aristocracy; they were chosen because they were not only wise, but could use their wisdom. They could give strength to the armies of the nation and they had the means of transmitting their power; for the Staff of the "King-Initiate" held so strong a magical potency, that, with it in his hand, the leader of armies became as mighty as Pharaoh himself.

The King-Priests gave forth an exoteric religion to the people, by which to guide their footsteps until they had reached that stage of development (it may have been only after repeated failures, incarnation after incarnation), when they also might join the ranks of the initiated: yet it appears extremely probable that the whole Egyptian population was allowed a certain participation in the Mysteries; for the tests of a candidate before Initiation were of such a nature that none but human beings developed to a considerable degree of perfection could hope to stand them.

There is every reason to suppose that only those who had received some grade of initiation were mummified; for it is certain that, in the eyes of the Egyptians, mummification effectually prevented reincarnation. Reincarnation was necessary to imperfect souls, to those who had failed to pass the tests of initiation; but for those who had the Will and the capacity to enter the Secret Adytum, there was seldom necessity for that liberation of the soul which is said to be effected by the destruction of the body.

The body of the Initiate was therefore preserved after death as a species of Talisman or material basis for the manifestation of the Soul upon earth.

In studying Egyptian Magic one has at once a thoroughly scientific satisfaction. One is troubled with no vague theories, but receives precise practical details; we observe that every square inch of the Upper and Under Worlds is mapped out. The strength that such a system inherently contains was proved by the long duration of the archaic Egyptian civilization.

The first principles of Egyptian Magic were based on an elaborate system of correspondences depending on the formula that, the evolution of what is material follows the type and symbol of the emanation of the spiritual; that spirit and matter are opposite faces of the self-same mystery.[2] The Egyptian Adepts regarded the conceptions of the mind, the aspirations of the soul, the words of the mouth and the functions of the body, as possessing analogies from which a complete system of rules of life and death could be constructed. Moreover they looked upon each body, or manifested being, as the material basis of a long vista of immaterial entities functioning as Spirit, Soul and Mind in the Formative, Creative and Archetypal Worlds.

Included in this volume is a list of standard works upon the subject of "Egyptian Beliefs," for the use of those who have not studied the modern theories on the subject; so there is no need to enter here into details which can easily be found elsewhere. I shall therefore at once state the ideas which my study of ancient lore has led me to formulate, without waiting to quote the hypotheses set forth by our leading Egyptologists.

In the first place we have hitherto written of man as composed of soul and body; but the Initiated Egyptians regarded themselves as being far from simply soul and body. They gave names to several human faculties, and postulated for each a possibility of separate existence.

The KHAT, KAT, or Body, was only a vehicle or material basis for the operations of the Ego upon this plane of human earth-life.

In considering the Egyptian philosophy of the Life Cycle, let us start from the beginning; according to the obelisk of Queen Hatshepsu, a human HAMMEMIT or Primal Entity circled round the sun for a period of One Hundred and Twenty Years before incarnation. During this period certain cosmic and elemental forces would be more powerful than others; these environing the Primal Entity would give it a certain characteristic bias, and guide it in the choice of the means and moment of incarnation. In the meantime the reflections of the higher elemental forces affecting the Primal Entity would be at work in the material world. These reflections would bias the human parents in like manner. When the natal epoch arrived the Great Mother-Force, symbolized by the vulture holding the Seal, imprinted upon the Primal Entity the symbols dominant at the selected moment; and this is the rationale of the Astrological horoscope.

The human mother had in the meantime become the centre of elemental forces that formulated an illusive attraction around her. This is the formulation of the SAHU, or the Astral body of the future human being, under the magic of the natural elemental forces. For the plainest woman, for a time, becomes beautiful in the eyes of her lover. No sooner, however, is the co-operation of the parent forces accomplished than the SAHU hastily attaches itself to the vitalized germ and remains with it as an invisible pattern towards which solid matter gravitating forms the material body. This operation of the SAHU accounts for the vision which some clairvoyants have perceived in regard to the Vegetable

Kingdom, of an astral plant-form attached to seeds or grains before they are sown in the ground.

The elemental body then having concentrated round the vitalized ovum, leaves the human mother in her natural state, stripped of the illusive beauty it had imparted to her: and she does not, or should not, regain her especially attractive power until she has done her part by the human being she is about to foster.

We see then that the unborn child is prepared for its emergence into life by the parents who contribute the principle called by the Egyptians the HATI or "whole heart." That is, the Seat of the Inherited instincts racial and individual; including such functions as digestion, hearing, seeing, smelling, and so on. In one word the HATI is the heredity. It is clothed by a body formulated by elemental forces, the SAHU. The SAHU, or astral body, both before and after conception, possessed that power of radiation which formed the sphere of attraction round the human mother, which was sealed by the great Vulture-Mother-Force at the time of conception, and was withdrawn instantly to form the sphere or aura of the future human being-this is called the KHAIBT, or radiating aura.

At the moment of birth the "Ego" joins the body, and there are extant many pictures (dating from the period of the highest Egyptian civilization) which show the birth of great princes; in these the double forms of the Celestially and Terrestrially generated bodies are recognisable. This is to say the circling HAMMEMIT now throws off an emanation which is called the KA or double of the new-born child, and this forms its link with the earthly body by means of another principle, the AB. The HATI is always spoken of in Egyptian texts as associated with the AB or Heart. Just as we, in our conversation, often confuse and combine our instinct and will. Will is a quality latent in every animal; it can in man be developed and cultivated until it becomes Free Will. In the same way the AB (will) or Red Vessel of the Heart is represented in the *Book of the Dead* as containing an egg, and a concave germ: when this concave germ is developed by cultivation the real life and full development of the Ego could begin: that is to say the KA could progress in its celestial evolution, just as the body could progress in its terrestrial evolution.

Of course in thousands of cases the celestial body was restricted; the fatal moment of conception loaded the terrestrial being (composed of the SAHU, HATI, and AB within the KAB or material body) with chains of destiny too strong for him to break through. And the KA or Ego had to return to the HAMMEMIT in the Place of Spirits and await the time when it might again have a chance of regenerating matter Astral and Material, and become of the number of these "Shining Ones," who are set like Jewels in the Diadem of the LORD OF SPIRIT AND LIFE, MADE ONE.

In this conception we have at once the explanation of the dogma regarding the sacrifice of self to self. For the KA or Ego can only grow and become potent through ardent and patient perseverance and struggle.

"Three days I hung upon the Cross, my Self a Sacrifice unto myself," says the God of the Eddas.

"Ich bin nichts in mir. Ichts in dir, und leben in deinem Ichts aus Nichts, lebe du doch in mir, und bringe mich aus dem Ichts in dir," said the German Mystic.[3]

The Man who cannot "be Himself" must be melted down in the casting-ladle of PHTHA. The artist-craftsman of the Gods will disperse the elemental material which in its present combination cannot, and will not, be regenerated; he bides his time for a happier moment of operation.

We have Christ enunciating this doctrine in the parable of the Talents, St. Luke, xix. 26, "Unto every one which hath shall be given, and from him that hath not, even that he hath shall be taken away from him."

This old Egyptian Doctrine is to be discovered again in Matthew Arnold's sonnet on "Immortality:"

"No, no, the energy of life may be
Kept on beyond the grave, but not begun,
And he who flagged not in the earthly strife
From strength to strength advancing, only he
His soul well-knit and all his battles won,
Mounts, and that hardly, to eternal life."

Having dwelt for some period on that dark side of the Egyptian Faith which dooms the impotent soul to extinction; I will proceed to discuss the career opened before those who, taking the reins of the chariot of life in their own hands, guide the elemental forces which are linked to that vehicle, safe to the desirable goal.

The seeds placed within the heart or Aʙ may now be considered as symbolising the powers of Thought and Will: these once set in action by Theurgic practices or self-devotion to the highest aspiration of the conscious being produce a curious result. Remembering that in the representations of the Aʙ the principles are reversed as though reflected in a vessel of blood—the concave germ being uppermost. We can then see that the two ends of the concave mass stretch round and form a receptacle for the egg: this symbolises a more quintessential influx from the primal entity or Hᴀᴍᴍᴇᴍɪᴛ descending upon the upstretched arms of the Kᴀ in the form of the Hawk or Bᴀɪᴇ. The Cultivation of Thought and Will is again shown by the uplifted hands in the hieroglyph which represents the Kᴀ: and the attitude of aspiration enables it to formulate a resting-place for the piercing, penetrating spirit, the Bᴀɪᴇ. This latter principle is represented in four ways; by a hawk crowned, or the Hᴏʀᴜs Bᴀɪᴇ; by a human-headed hawk; by a Bennu bird or by a ram. The Bᴀɪᴇ (spirit) can operate through the egg-like principle contained in the Aʙ and the Kᴀ (human Ego) through the concave principle.

These four hieroglyphs used for the word Bᴀɪᴇ showed distinct orders or genera of souls; for instance, the hawk-soul is only represented as resting upon the Kᴀ of the King or Queen. It is called the Royal Soul. The human-headed hawk hovers over the mummies of great initiates and doubtless represents the soul after the incarnation had ceased; its human head is the symbol of the quintessence of the human individuality which the bird bears to the Abode of Blessed Souls.

The BAIE represented by the ram would be the progressive, penetrating power which breaks down barriers and enables the energised human soul to pass into regions, the guardians of which could hold their own against meeker enquiry.

The Bennu bird also is remarkable for transfixing and piercing its prey. There is considerable difficulty about this hieroglyph; if it represents the phœnix as it has been commonly supposed to do, it would be easy to understand that it was the symbol of a soul belonging to a more complex range of being, only to be evolved through a long series of labours on the part of its human counterpart; but if it is simply a form of a common hernshaw[4] I should take it as implying a milder and less fiery nature in the soul.

The ram head is often placed on the stone scarabæus (symbol of self-creation) which replaces the heart in the body of a mummy; representing what the mediæval mystics meant when they talked of the "Stone of the Wise." That is, the Will which had become self-creative and was united eternally to its celestial, progressive, penetrative faculty. The consecrated Will and purified Thought of the true Magus.

In the first Egyptian Room at the British Museum a painting, said to be of Queen Hatshepset, who lived about 1600 B.C., is hung on the walls (the Queen's name has been painted out and that of Thothmes III substituted), she is making perfume offerings; this picture is reproduced from an obelisk now fallen, which was set up by this Queen at Karnak. A print of this painting is reproduced in the English translation of Wiedemann's *Immortality of the Soul.*

Here we have a representation of a fully initiated ruler. Her Divine Powers are represented on her head-dress by the feathers of the Celestial and Terrestrial Truth; the orb of the Sun; the two Goddesses ruling the commencement and the fruition, represented by the horned and orbed uræii, symbols of beauty, life, and fierce protective motherhood; the ram›s horns of all-penetrating potency; the nemyss with the fiery serpent of prophecy and protection upright before her face.

Above the figure of the Queen is the Mother-vulture; at once the avenging, protective, and intuitive emissary of Maut the Mother of all things; holding the Seal composed of a ring and a plate engraved with the symbols of the birth-presiding forces which gave a name of power to the Queen.

Behind her is her Ka or real Ego; the hands, lifted in aspiration above the head, enclose the rectangular parallelogram representing the Portal of Wisdom in which is written the Horus or heroic Name which according to Egyptian dogma was to be won by the Theurgic rites of Initiation. On it is seated the Royal Horus Baie. In the hands of the Ka is the Staff or Magical Wand which, rightly understood, was a means of transmitting the Royal Power to such of her subjects as she selected to carry out her Will.

Proclus in *Timœus* book v., page 330 says, speaking of the Baie, Spirit:

"Her seeds are hurled into the realms of generation; and she must purify herself from circumjacent fluctuations of matter. For she contains two-fold powers, one leading to generation the other from generation to true being. The one leads her round the Genesiurgic, the other round the intellectual circle."

In this way we come to the consideration of the magical Power of the Soul: called by the Egyptians the Yekh, Khou or Shining One. We find in nearly all the Magical Tales that it was through the initiative of the Khou that really magical acts were performed. M.F. Chabas in his supplement to the *Harris Magical Papyrus* gives many instances of the good and evil uses made of the Khou.

One entered the body of a princess who was obsessed for a long period, until it was cast out by means of the health-giving Divinity.

It was the Khou which had been degraded that became a demon and the torturer of mankind. The fate of such was to sacrifice the negatively evil, those who had neglected their opportunities; but the evil KHOUS could not themselves be annihilated. An evil immortality awaited the great evil-doer or destroyer among mankind; just as a beautiful immortality awaited the Shining Ones who had added to the beauty of life in their mortal days. Between these extremes of beauty and destruction lay the impotent and the ignorant, whose blindness doomed them to annihilation.

The beatitude of the Justified KHOU was by no means purely contemplative. The inscription on the obelisk of Queen Hatshepsu (sometimes spelled Hatshepset) speaks of them as holding converse with the ungenerated souls during the one hundred and twenty years that the latter circle round the Sun. They had the power to take all imaginable forms, or to move hither and thither as they pleased.

We find in the *Ritual of the Dead* elaborate formulas for the assistance of the KHOU of the deceased. The Justified KHOU was obliged to pass many tests; it had to cultivate the gardens of heaven, destroy monsters, take on certain obligatory forms, escort the Gods in their Heaven-traversing ships, take part in the ceaseless struggle between the two contending forces, cross burning and desolate zones, suffer in the regions of hunger, thirst, and terror, submit to proofs; reply to questions, and pass the armed and hideous Deity who guarded the Portals of Wisdom.

Now, if an Egyptian failed in standing such tests as these, in the ceremony of his initiation, he was regarded as a man liable to become an evil KHOU if his power was developed: and in their Wisdom the Priests rejected him and left him in that ignorance which led to oblivion and the annihilation of the incarnating Ego. Not only this, but if he, by underhand means, found out magical formulas and was able to use them effectively, the punishment was death.

Details of this kind are given in the supplement to M. Chabas' translation of the *Harris Magical Papyrus*. The period was that of Rameses III. Compare this quotation:

"HAI, the evil man, was a shepherd. He had said:—

'Oh! that I might have a book of spells that would give me resistless power.'

He obtained a book of the Formulas of Rameses-Meri-Amen, the Great God, his royal Master. By the Divine Powers of these, he enchanted men. He obtained a deep vault furnished with implements. He made waxen images of men, and love-charms. And then he perpetrated all the horrors that his heart conceived."

Now on the face of the matter it is very easy to see that a great part of Egyptian Magic lay in a species of Hypnotism, called by later magicians, Enchantment, Fascination, and so forth. Anybody with intelligence and charm can hypnotise an innocent person that interests him, but such a practice is derogatory both to fascinator and fascinated, even when it takes place in matters of ordinary passional life. How much more so when it leads to debauchery of the soul. In this way we perceive the possibility of an Uninitiate successfully performing the spells he had discovered.

Rituals or Ceremonies now simply regarded as a waste of time by those who have to assist at their celebration, had a potent effect when the symbolism of each action was fully recognised, and when the imagination was extended and ultra-sensitive, and the Will concentrated firmly and repeatedly, on the object to be accomplished. The KA of the Ritualist was thus at high tension acting upon its counterpart the concave germ in the AB (heart) or vessel of conscious desire; this reacts upon the HATI (Instinctive habit) or unconscious executant. The whole human Ego then being in a state of theurgic excitation the BAIE (Spirit) descended and the whole being became a luminous KHOU or Shining Body of super-human potency, the Augoeides of the Greek Mystics.

This glittering being established in the midst of the SAHU (Elemental Body) then by its radiation can awake corresponding potencies in nature. For this purpose the KHAIBT was used as a link between the Ego and the non-Ego, and the spiritual body or ZET was established.

When this condition was brought about, a man became in the eyes of the Egyptians, Osirified. That is to say, a Microprosopus, or Perfect copy of the Macroprosopus. But he who, ignorant and unpurified, performed these rites, became the habitation of an illusive and fatal force, ever dragging him down to the deep abysses of blind potency.

We may now perceive dimly how the Egyptians conceived the seed of the Tree of Life-Eternal to be implanted in the heart of each man or woman born on earth; how it can wither and fade; how it can be cultivated until the man becomes either an Evil Demon or a God.

To the high initiate there was no question of choice in this matter. He knew that the heart turned inward on itself and it was a very poor alternative for that expansion of being that belongs to the development of the whole latent Divine Powers of the Microprosopus. In other words, the perfect formulation of the Osiris soul, the Holy Spirit of the Divine, made manifest and eternal.

Now the Egyptians had elaborated a marvellous system of symbolism. The forms of the universal powers or Gods, stood, each complete, behind a human or animal mask; his Divinity symbolized by his headdress, his powers by his Staff and the Symbol of Life which he bore in his hands. M. Chabas and Textor de Ravisi have told us that the most potent magical formula was the identification of the Ritualist with the God whose power he was invoking. So increasing himself to an immeasurable greatness he leapt beyond all bodies, and transcending time became eternity. He became higher than all height, lower than all depth. He knew himself part of the great chain of Creation at once unbegotten, young, old, dead. He felt within himself latent, unfolding faculties, and retained the memory of experiences gained in time long past and dead. His feet to-day stood in the place that yesterday his eye could scarcely see, and beyond him in the Invisible was his next day's resting place.

In the sixty-fourth chapter of the *Book of the Dead,* dating back to the IVth dynasty about 3733 B.C., the rubric tells us that:

"If this chapter is known the person is made triumphant upon earth, and in the nether world, and he performeth all things that are done by the living. This composition is a secret—not to be seen or looked at. Recite the chapter when sanctified and pure, not approaching women, not eating goats' flesh or fish."

The text contains the following passages:

"I am Yesterday, To-day and To-morrow, for I am born again and again. I am That Whose Force is unmanifest and nourisheth the Dwellers in the West. I am the Guider in the East. The Lord of the Two Faces Who seeth by His own Light. The Lord of Resurrections Who cometh forth from the Dusk and Whose Birth is from the House of Death.

Ye Two Divine Hawks upon your stations; Watchers of the Material World; ye who go with the bier to its eternal home, and ye who conduct the Ship of the Sun; advancing onwards from the highest Heaven to the place of the Sarcophagus.

This is the Lord of the Shrine which standeth in the centre of the Earth, He is in me; and I am in Him.

Mine is the radiance in which PHTHA floateth over His Firmament.

Oh! Sun Who smileth gladly, and whose heart is delighted with the perfect Order of this day as thou enterest into Heaven and earnest forth in the East: the Ancients and those Who are gone before, acclaim thee!

Let thy paths be made pleasant for me.

Let thy ways be made wide for me to traverse the earth and the expanse of Heaven. Shine Thou upon me, O penetrating power, as I draw near to the Divine Words my ears shall hear in the Abodes of the West. Let no pollution of that which brought me forth be upon me. Deliver me, protect me from him who closeth His Eyes at twilight and bringeth to an end in darkness. (The annihilator.)

I am He Who bursteth the Bonds. Uttermost Extension is my Name. I bring to its fulness the Force which is hidden within me."

.   .   .   .   .

"I am He Who cometh forth as One Who breaketh open the Gates: and Everlasting is the Daylight which His Will hath created. I know (I have power over) the Deep Waters, is my Name."

.   .   .   .   .

"I shine forth as the Lord of Life and the glorious Law of Light."

.   .   .   .   .

"I come as the Ambassador of the Lord of Lords to avenge the cause of Osiris in this Place. Let the Eye consume its tears. I am the Guide to the House of Him Who dwelleth in His Treasures."

.   .   .   .   .

"I travel on high, I tread upon the Firmament, I raise a flame with the lightning which mine eye hath made, and I fly forward towards the Splendours of the Glorified in the presence of the Sun, who daily giveth Life to every man who walketh about the habitations of the earth.

Oh! Thou who leapest forth! Conductor of the Shades and the glorified Ones from the earth! Let the fair path to the Western Abodes, which is made in behalf of those who faint, and for the restoration of those who are in pain, be granted unto me.

Blessed are they who see the bourne. Beautiful is the God of the motionless heart, who restoreth Peace to the Torrent.

Behold! There cometh forth the Lord of Life, Osiris, Thy support who abideth day and night."

.   .   .   .   .

"I fly up to heaven and I alight upon earth and mine eye turneth back towards the traces of my footsteps. I am the offspring of yesterday. The caverns of the earth have given me birth, and I am revealed at my appointed time."

This is the Triumphant Death-Song of the Initiated Egyptian. To Him the Life beyond the grave—the abodes of the West—opened a wider range of activity. To him Initiation meant the hastening of the Time of Ripened Power when he might become One with the Great God of Humanity, Osiris; slain that he might rise again, perfected through suffering, glorified through humiliation.

This was the highest work of magic, the Spiritual Alchemy or the Transmutation from human Force to Divine Potency. As is said by the great Iamblichus, in section iv., chapter ii., of *The Mysteries:*

"The Priest who invokes is a man; but when he commands powers it is because through arcane symbols, he, in a certain respect, is invested with the sacred Form of the Gods."

Iamblichus also tells us that the daimon or elemental ruler is received at the hour of birth. It is a personification of the Symbol imprinted on the SAHU or Elemental body; and its action may be defined as that of Fate or Destiny. Its forces are drawn from the whole world, and it is established in the SAHU before the soul descends into generation. He says further: —

"And when the soul has received Him as her leader the Daimon immediately presides over the soul, gives completion to its lives, and binds it to body when it descends. He likewise governs the common animal of the soul (the Sahu) and directs its peculiar life, and imparts to us the principles of all our thought and reasonings. We also perform such things as he suggests to our intellect, and he continues to govern us till, through sacerdotal theurgy, we obtain a God for the inspective guardian and leader of the soul. For then the Daimon either yields or delivers his government to a more excellent nature, or is subjected to him as contributing to his guardianship, or in some other way is ministrant to him as to his Lord."

When this takes place, and the body, sealed by destiny, is made subject, by initiation, to the Divine Powers, it may well be symbolised by the Ka supporting the Baie on the portal of initiation. The Lower Self being sacrificed to the Higher Self. The Osiris Man is established, as in the symbols in which the Osiris is represented by the Tat or Symbol of Stability. Then, and then only, is the question of Sacrifice for others to be considered. And the Osiris may plunge once again into matter; once again making use of his mummified form to seek and to save that which was lost.

Mild saintliness was by no means the ideal of the Egyptian Priesthood. Intense practical interest in the life of their country, and the ennobling of natural functions, drew a sharp contrast between them and the ascetics of India and Christendom. "Whatever your hand findeth to do; do it with your might," is a text that may well have come down to us from Ancient Egypt. The generative processes of Nature were honoured by them at special festivals—but at the same time the degradation of natural functions by excess was sternly reprimanded.

The Laws of Moses were to a great extent derived from the Laws of Ancient Egypt, and whatever else may be said of them they certainly tend to sanitary conditions, and length of life, individual and racial.

Now we know that with the Jews Magic was practised in the Sanctuary, but denounced by the Priesthood; it was only when Saul found the Sacred Oracles of the *Urim* and *Thummim* deaf to his questions that he consulted a mistress of the Aub or Astral Light.—I Samuel xxviii., v. 7.

So in Egypt we find side by side with the high Theurgic mysteries (of which a good idea may be formed from the writings of Iamblichus), a more material development of Magical Art.

Notes:
1. Reprinted from *Egyptian Magic* by S.S.D.D. [Florence Farr.] Theosophical Publishing Society, 1896.—D.K.
2. See W. Wynn Westcott on "Kabbalah," in *Lucifer,* May, 1893. p. 204, and Tyndall, Belfast Address.—S.S.D.D.
3. "I am nothing in myself. Nothing in you, and nothing out of nothing in your life, but you live in me and bring me out of nothing in you."—D.K.
4. A "hernshaw" is a variant of British dialect for a heronsew or heron.—D.K.

LIST OF BOOKS FOR REFERENCE

Egyptian Beliefs

ADAMS, (W. MARSHAM):—The House of the Hidden Places. A clue to the Creed of Early Egypt from Egyptian Sources. Cloth, 8vo. London, 1895.

AMELINEAU, (M.E.):—Essai sur L'Evolution, historique et philosophique, des idées morales dans l'Egypte Ancienne. Wrappers, 8vo. Paris, 1895.

AMELINEAU, (M.E.):—Essai sur le Gnosticisme Egyptien, ses développements et son origine Egyptienne. Wrappers, 4to. Paris, 1887.

AMELINEAU (M.E.):—Notice sur le Papyrus Gnostique Bruce. Texte et Traduction. Wrappers, 4to. Paris, 1891.

AMELINEAU (M.E.):—Histoire de la Sépulture et des Funérailles dans l'Ancienne Egypte. Avec nombreuses vignettes et 112 planches hors texte. First series. Wrappers, 4to. Two vols. Paris, 1896.

BONOMI (JOSEPH) and SHARPE (SAMUEL):—The Alabaster Sarcophagus of Oimenepthah I., King of Egypt. Beautifully illustrated. Boards, 4to. London, 1864.

BOOK OF THE DEAD:—Facsimile of the Papyrus of Ani in the British Museum. Second edition. With thirty-seven coloured double plates. Folio. London.

BUDGE (E.A. WALLIS):—Book of the Dead. Reprint of the Egyptian text of the papyrus of Ani in the British Museum, with interlinear transliteration, and an English literal translation, a running translation, an introduction and notes. cxxxii, and 377 pp. 4to half calf. 1895.

The introduction contains chapters on the versions of the *Book of the Dead* ; The Legend of Osiris ; the Doctrine of Eternal Life ; Egyptian ideas of God; the Abode of the Blessed; the Gods of the *Book of the Dead;* Geographical and Mythological Places; Funeral Ceremonies, *etc.*

BUDGE (E.A. WALLIS):—An Egyptian Reading Book for Beginners. Cloth, thick, 8vo. London, 1896.

BUDGE (E.A. WALLIS):—First Steps in Egyptian. A Book for Beginners. Cloth, 8vo. London, 1895.

BUDGE (E.A. WALLIS):—The Sarcophagus of Anchnesrāneferāb, Queen of Ahmes II., King of Egypt. Text and Translation. Cloth, 4to. London, 1885.

BRIMMER (MARTIN):—Egypt. Three Essays on the History, Religion and Art of Ancient Egypt. Beautifully illustrated. Leather, 8vo. Cambridge, U.S.A., 1892.

CHABAS (M. François-Joseph):—Le Papyrus Magique Harris. Wrappers, 4to. Chalons-sur-Saone, 1860.

CORY (J.P.):—Ancient Fragments of the Phœnician, Carthaginian, Babylonian and other Authors. New edition by E. Richmond Hodges. Cloth, 8vo. London, 1876.

DIVINE PYMANDER OF HERMES. Translated by Dr. Everard. Preface by Dr. W. Wynn Westcott. Cloth, 8vo. London, 1894.

ERMAN (ADOLF):—Egyptian Grammar with table of signs, bibliography, exercises for reading, and glossary. Translated by J.H. Breasted. Cloth, 8vo. London, 1894.

KING (C.W.):—The Gnostics and Their Remains, Ancient and Mediæval. Second Edition. Illustrated. Cloth, 8vo. London, 1887.

KING (C.W.):—Plutarch's Morals. Theosophical Essays. Cloth, 8vo. London, 1889. Contains a translation of the famous treatise on "Isis and Osiris."

LE PLONGEON (A):—Queen Móo and the Egyptian Sphinx. Illustrated. Cloth, 8vo. New York, 1896.

LOCKYER (J. NORMAN):—The Dawn of Astronomy. A Study of the Temple-Worship and Mythology of the Ancient Egyptians. Cloth, 8vo. London, 1894.

MAHAFFY (J. P.):—The Empire of the Ptolemies. Cloth, 8vo. London, 1895.

MALLET (D.):—Le Culte de Neit à Sais, étude de Mythologie Egyptienne. Wrappers, 8vo. Paris, 1888.

MASPERO (G.):—The Dawn of Civilization. Egypt and Chaldæa. Illustrated. Second Edition, revised and brought up to date. Cloth, 4to. London, 1896.

MASPERO (G.):—Life in Ancient Egypt and Assyria, with one hundred and eighty-eight illustrations. Cloth, 8vo. London, 1892.

MASPERO (G.):—Manual Of Archæology and Guide to the Study of Antiquities in Egypt, with three hundred and nine illustrations. Cloth, 8vo. London, 1895.

MEAD (G.R.S.):—Orpheus. Cloth, 8vo. London, 1896.

MEAD (G.R.S.):—Pistis Sophia. A Gnostic Gospel (with extracts from the Books of the Saviour appended). Translated with an introduction. Cloth, 8vo. London, 1896.

PETRIE (W.M. FLINDERS):—A History of Egypt from the earliest times to the XVI. Dynasty. With numerous illustrations. Cloth, 8vo. Two vols. London, 1896.

PETRIE (W.M. FLINDERS):—Egyptian Tales, translated from the Papyri. illustrated. Cloth, 8vo. First and second series.

PIERRET (PAUL):—Le Livre des Morts. Traduction du rituel Funeraire Egyptien. Wrappers, 8vo. Paris, 1882.

PIERRET (PAUL):—Le Pantheon Egyptien. Illustrated. Wrappers, 8vo. Paris, 1880.

RENOUF (P. LE PAGE):—Book of the Dead. [The Egyptian.] Being a complete translation, commentary, and notes. Small 4to. London, 1893-96. To be completed in eight parts, of which five are already published.

RENOUF (P. LE PAGE):—The Religion of Ancient Egypt. Cloth, 8vo. London, 1893.

SHARPE (SAMUEL):—Egyptian Mythology and Egyptian Christianity, with their influence on the opinions of Modern Christendom. Cloth, 8vo. London, 1896.

TAYLOR (THOMAS):—Jamblichus on the Mysteries of the Egyptians, Chaldeans and Assyrians. Translated from the Greek. Cloth, 8vo. London. 1895.

TAYLOR (THOMAS):—The Mystical Hymns of Orpheus. Translated from the Greek, and demonstrated to be the Invocations used in the Eleusinian Mysteries. Cloth, 8vo. London, 1896.

WIEDEMANN (ALFRED):—The Ancient Egyptian Doctrine of the Immortality of the Soul. With twenty-one illustrations. Cloth, 8vo. London, 1895.

An Introduction to Alchemy.[1]

By V.H. Soror S.S.D.D.

Writers on Alchemy are in the habit of making so many prefatory remarks on their own account, that their books stand in very little need of preface; unless indeed, the Editor undertakes to reveal the secrets which the Author is so careful to conceal. I must at once say I am not prepared to do this, but to one thing, I can with advantage call your attention, which is that the study of Alchemy, above all other branches of Occult Science, demonstrates the value of Analogy in our search after the real meaning of the mysteries of man and his relation to the Universe. The process of transmutation, which displays a series of colours, recalls the Religion of the Egyptians, symbolising as it did, the blackness of night, the rainbow colours of dawn, the whiteness of noon, and the red glow of evening. The first stage of this symbolism alludes to the blackness of ignorance, the chaotic darkness of men who reject the keys to the secret of the Universe, which are to be found in the rainbow colours; to the vibrations of sound, to scents, tastes, feelings, and subtle psychical impressions. When a man's mind begins to grasp the order and reration of such sense impressions as these, he bids fair to pass from the darkness of ignorance to the white light of wisdom, and perhaps eventually to attain to the imperial purple which clothes the elect.

To do this he must, within himself, possess the divine gift of *wonder*; for it is through this faculty that he raises himself above the cares of life. The man whose curiosity carries him from the contemplation of the manifestation to the contemplation of its causes, is the man whose instincts are preparing him to undertake the Great Work.

Content is fatal; the man who is content with anything, who does not feel in his most successful moments, during the most sacred earthly joys, a keen sense of want and disappointment, can never hope to find the Stone of the Wise—true wisdom and perfect happiness.

The happy are sufficiently rare, however, for me to hope that few of my readers will be deterred from the study of Alchemy by what I have said. We have all been taught to look with horror upon Medusa's head, with the serpents twisting round its face, the terror of which turned all to stone who gazed upon it. But we must, if we would learn the secret wisdom of the ages, learn to long for a glance from those wonderful eyes, which will bestow upon us the gift of indifference to personal joys and sorrows. For the wise man must be as a precious stone; a centre of light to all that approach him; giving joy to others, because he contains the image of the highest joy in himself; desiring nothing from the world, drawing his inspiration from the supernal light—that "Wisdom Goddess" who wears the serpent crowned head upon her shield.

Well has Robert Fludd said, "Be ye changed from dead stones into living philosophical stones. Be equal with God. Ye hear all these things but ye believe not. Oh miserable mortals, who do so anxiously, run after your own ruin."

Then the philosopher points out the futility of the ordinary man of petty aims and weak will, never gaining the goal of the higher, or for the matter of that, the lower Alchemy.

"Oh thou miserable one, wilt thou be more happy?

Oh thou proud one, wilt thou be elevated above the circles of this world?

Oh thou ambitious one, wilt thou command in Heaven above this earth, and thy dark body?

Oh ye unworthy, will ye perform all miracles?

Know ye rejected ones, of what nature it is, before ye seek it."

So it comes to the old, old teaching, GNOTHI SEAUTON, Know thyself; until by deep thought and meditation, words have become more than words to thee; until thou hast analyzed them, separated them, transposed them into every conceivable form, and finally extracted from them, their quintessence and spiritual meaning, thou wilt understand no word that the ancient philosophers speak to thee.

Take now the loose meaning attached to such a word as imagination; in these materialistic days it has become synonymous with extravagant fancy, if not with lying: but hear what Paracelsus says of imagination as an occult manifestation of power: "Man has a visible and invisible workshop. The visible one is his body, the invisible one his imagination. . . . The imagination is a sun in the soul of man acting in its own sphere, as the sun in our system acts on the earth. Wherever the latter shines, germs planted in the soil grow, and vegetation springs up; the imagination acts in a similar manner m the soul, and calls forms of life into existence. . . . The Spirit is the master, imagination the tool; and the body the plastic material. Imagination is the power by which the will forms sidereal entities out of thoughts, it can produce and cure disease."

Perhaps this passage will give new light to those who have lately treated this faculty with such contempt, in dealing with the subject of hypnotism.

In truth, Imagination is the power of forming images in our minds. It is the development and intensification of an idea, which first exists, is then conceived passively in the thought sphere; then the mind (perceiving the idea can be used) brings desire into play, which is developed into an act of Will, and this converts the passive conception of the idea into an active Imagination. So begins the magical process, the rest it is not for me to divulge.

I will only add on this subject the saying of Eliphaz Levi, that, "The first matter of the Magnum Opus is both within and about us, and the intelligent will, which assimilates light, directs the operations of substantial form, and only employs chemistry as a very secondary instrument."

The *Suggestive Enquiry*,[2] published a century later than the work under our consideration, points out the method which should be employed in the exhaustive analysis of the nature of man, so necessary to the completion of the great work. He says:—

"Metempsychosis takes the human identity (or consciousness) from animal existence to the ethereal elements of its original formation."

That is, in thinking inwardly with calm and philosophic mind we can pass from the manifested life we see and feel, to the motive power of that life; and finally to the cause of the motive power; from the mundane to the supra-mundane; from the intellectual to the intelligible; from the earth to the firmament; from water to the fiery rays of heat emerging from the central light which is the source of all things.

The same book continues, "These elements are the universal fundamentals of nature: only in the Human form can they attain that supremacy of reason which returns to its first cause."

Reason is the light which guides us. Let me hasten to add how necessary it is to distinguish between the false reason, and the Heavenly Reason which we perceive when intuition is purified; and we rise above the lower passions. The false reason is merely an image set up by our unbalanced forces to justify us in evil doing. Well has it been said, that when we find ourselves seeking to justify ourselves by giving reasons for our actions, we have been doing something we are secretly ashamed of.

True Reason is the clear light descending upon us from that which is above all pretence. It was a communion with this faculty, that Saint Thomas à Kermpis desired when he told those who would detain him, he must leave them, as one was waiting for him in his cell. False reason seeks to justify itself with much argument; Pure Reason knows Truth, and can afford to be silent.

So continues the *Suggestive Enquiry*, "In the Human form only is it possible to comprehend the Divine form; when it has done so by a triplicate growth of Light in the understanding consciously allied, it emanates a fourth form, truthful, godlike, being the express image of its person magically portrayed."

I think I have said enough to show that the Alchemist undertakes no light task. I can hold out no hope of success to those who still retain an absorbing interest in the world. *In the world Adepts may be, but not of* it. Alchemy is a jealous mistress, she demands from pupils no less than life; for her sake you must perform the twelve labours of Hercules; for her you must descend into Hell, for her sake you must ascend into Heaven. You must have strength and patience, nothing must terrify you, the joys of Nirvâna must not tempt you; having chosen your work, you must to this end purify yourself from perishable desires, and bring down the light of the shining ones, that it may radiate upon you here on earth. This is the work of the Alchemist; his true ideal is also the highest ideal of Eastern Theosophy; to choose a life that shall bring him in touch with the sorrows of his race rather than accept the Nirvâna open to him; and like other Saviours of the world, to remain manifested as a living link between the supernal and terrestrial natures.

S.S.D.D.–R.R. *et* A.C.

Notes:
1. Reprinted from *A Short Enquiry concerning the Hermetic Art* by A Lover of Philalethes. Theosophical Publishing Society, [1894].–D.K.
2. *A Suggestive Inquiry into the Hermetic Mystery with a Dissertation on the More Celebrated of the Alchemical Philosophers, Being an Attempt Towards the Recovery of the Ancient Experiment of Nature* [by Mary Anne Atwood]. London: Trelawney Saunders, 1850. This book was originally published anonymously, but the Author's name first appeared in the 1918 edition (London: W. Tait).–D.K.

Commentary on Euphrates;
or, the Waters of the East.[1]

By S.S.D.D.

LET no man take up this book in the hope of finding it to contain a treatise on the transmutation of metals. It is rather a very profitable study of the philosophy of nature and a guide to the attainment of that perfection of mind and body, which has been called by some, the achievement of Adeptship.

Thomas Vaughan, who wrote under the name of Eugenius Philalethes, the lover of truth, published this work in 1655. At a time when the struggles between Puritans and Catholics had reached an acute stage. At a time when it was dangerous to write openly, and when man was still supposed to be the end of Creation. Spinoza was writing his exposure of the ignorance of Bible commentators and of the vulgar interpretation of the Scriptures; Hume's famous essay on miracles was still unthought of; Nature was degraded as the enemy of God much in the same way as Woman was looked upon as the temptress of Man.

Luther's demand that the "sacred oracles" should be placed in the hands of the unlearned, while it exposed the restrictions of the Priestly teaching was still doing as much harm as good. For without much learning, the words of the Jewish scriptures may be twisted into enough contradictory dogmas to furnish the battle cries of opposing sects till the end of time.

It is impossible to understand the Old Testament while we are ignorant of the esoteric construction put upon it by the Jews; and this key to its secret meaning is given in the Kabbalah. That Thomas Vaughan was a Kabbalist there is no doubt; but he dared not openly acknowledge the fact; so that we shall find him frequently speaking in a manner that obliges him to excuse himself to the learned and acknowledge that he writes thus "for the sake of those with weak consciences."

Our author says that he treats of a "subject which is universal;" that is to say, of a subject which has its analogies on all planes, a subject "which is the *foundation* of all nature."

Now the Foundation was the special name used by English Kabbalists to translate the word Yesod, which is the Ninth Sephirah, or absolute emanation of the manifesting God; and the waters of the fourth river of Eden, Phrath or Euphrates, flow down through the foundation of life into the visible universe.

The Egyptians, in whose secret archives we find the origin of much of the Kabbalah, considered the human principle, or Chaibt, which they represented hieroglyphically by an open fan, to imply the emanation known to moderns as the odour, or the Aura, or the sympathetic or antipathetic influence of one being upon another.

In like manner we may think of the Sephirah Yesod as not only a symbol of generative force, but also of this subtle emanation acting and reacting upon all creation; some of the results of which are tides, tempests, affinities, love, friendship; which is in fact the foundation alike of the relationship of a being to its parts, and of one being to another.

This odour or Aura is especially noticeable in vegetable life. It is found that the essential oil existing in the outer cells of the petals is the source of the perfume of a flower, the lower surfaces containing tannin and colouring matter. Now the first action of the Foundation of life is to emit an odorous sphere or aura or emanation of influence. From the interaction of this with the Ruach or spirit, the material body is formulated from the elements. The seed being the magnet of attraction as we shall see expressed later on in the text of this work.

Thomas Vaughan's next sentence confirms us in the conclusion that the ideas he associates with the word Foundation are strictly

Kabbalistic, "That is the matter whereof all things are made, and wherewith being made they are nourished."

Now there is no doubt that in whatever form we may take our food, whether as beef, rice, or green food, it is alike resolved by digestion and fermentation into a milky emulsion in which will be found the essential oils of the various ingredients we have eaten, and that occurs before it can in any way be said to nourish us.

Again Metals can be acted upon by ferments of an acid nature and so changed into their higher form or tincture, but without the aid of the external elementary substance they are in themselves incapable of regeneration.

Having said thus much in words intended to puzzle the untrained scholar, our author closes his introduction abruptly, advising the student to apply himself to physic, or the regeneration of his own nature rather than to the making of gold.

With a final warning against metals and an exhortation to seek only the first mixture of elements which nature makes, he closes his introduction.

I may here remark that after fermentation or putrefaction, an amount of a volatile oil far exceeding in quantity the original essential oil of a natural substance can be extracted from it by the usual processes of distillation, *etc.*

Fermentation in this sense was one of the most important processes known to the ancients.

We may I think gather that the essential oil and comprehend with it the perfume or aura, was the physical basis of life in the eyes of the ancients. Death, putrefaction or fermentation sets free large quantities of this essence which when treated by the wise, may effect the regeneration of a particular body. Bringing about by art in a short time what nature would have effected slowly.

COMMENTS UPON THE FIRST PARAGRAPH.

"And I heard the Angel of the Waters say, Thou art righteous, O Lord, which art, and wast, and shalt be, because thou hast judged thus." (Rev. xvi. 5.)

Here we find at once our author falling in with the "weak consciences" he expected to deal with, and for the moment taking the literal meaning of the *seared oracles*.

"For an angel went down at a certain season into the pool and troubled the water." (St. John v. 4.)

"And the Spirit of God moved upon the face of the waters." (Gen. i. 2.)

Then he circumstantially states his opinion that God's Work does not disgrace God's Word, and his object is "to show that God is conversant with matter though he be not tied to it." It is curious to note that Professor Tyndal in his famous Belfast Address to the British Association for the Advancement of Science made an almost identical appeal to his audience saying:—

"Spirit and matter have ever been presented to us in the rudest contrast, the one as all noble, the other as all-vile. Supposing that, instead of having the foregoing antithesis of spirit and matter presented to our youthful minds, we had been taught to regard them as equally worthy and equally wonderful; to consider them as two opposite faces of the self-same mystery. ... Looking at matter not as brute matter but as the living garment of God; do you not think the law of relativity might have had an outcome different from its present one? Without this total Revolution of the notions now prevalent, the Evolution hypothesis must stand condemned (for what is the core, the essence of this hypothesis? Strip it naked and you stand face to face with the notion that not the more ignoble forms of animalculæ, but the human body, the human mind itself, emotion, intellect, will, and all their phenomena were once latent in a fiery cloud); but in many profoundly thoughtful minds such a revolution has already taken place. They degrade neither member of the mysterious duality referred to, but they exalt one of them from its abasement, and repeal the divorce hitherto existing between both. In substance, if not in words, their position as regards the relation of spirit and matter is; 'What God hath joined together let not man put asunder.'"

It is necessary in this place to make a slight digression on the nature of God according to the Ancients. "The Egyptians recognised a divinity only in those cases where they perceived a fixed law either of permanence or change. The Earth abides, so do the Heavens, Days, Months, Seasons; these show a regularity which was called Maät. The Gods are called possessors of Maät or subsisting through Maät. Truth and Justice are but forms of Maät applied to human action.» (Renouf, Introduction to the *Papyrus of Ani.*) Beyond these the Egyptians believed in the Unnameable One. He whose throne the plumes of Amen's head-dress barely touch. (The Hebrew root Amen, AMN, signifies stability.)

Among the Jews, the "Jehovah" holy as He was, existed only as the manifesting deity taking form in the world of matter as the holy living creatures, the forces of heat, moisture, cold and dryness; or on another plane developing as spirit, soul, mind and matter. But the real Being of Deity was called "Ehyeh," the "I am that I am," and behind Him was the Potential Being or Ain Soph Aur. For it is Written "His is the Mind, theirs are the powers" [in the *Chaldæan Oracles*].[2]

In the same way Brahma the Universe separated its body into two halves; *Viraj*, the spiritual, intelligent nature, and *Vach* or the manifest expression of the eternal divine Ideation. But this was not the same as the Great Brahm, or "Great Breath" breathing out for millions of years, and again breathing in for the same period, becoming alternately manifest and unmanifest. So far we have spoken of the Macrocosmic God or Macroprosopus. Of the Microprosopus; the Microcosmic God of the New Testament, He through whom we can approach the vast ideal which the human brain is too small to grasp, we need not here speak further.

I must now deal shortly with the occult meaning of the Fall. The Fall means more especially—fallen into generation or corruptibility. When Isis let loose Typhon after his imprisonment by Horus, her enraged son destroyed her royal diadem and cut off her head, but Thoth—in one sense the moon god, replaced it by a cow's head. That is to say, when in the course of cosmic evolution Primæval chaos seemed to return as ruler of night and winter, the child of the spirit moving on the waters of creation laid low the glorious mother who had borne him. She, became the Nature Goddess of the earth the symbol of fruitfulness, the sacred cow, the increaser of harvest. Henceforth the processes of change became recognised as gods or "fixed laws;" death and corruption which for a time seem like annihilation, being some of these.

Of the teaching of the Kabbalah on the Fall I have only room to quote the following paragraph from S.L. Macgregor Mathers› Introduction to the *Kabbalah Unveiled*:—

> "The first two letters of Jehovah, I and H, are the father and mother of Microprosopus" (or the supernal Adam) "and the H final is his bride" (or Eve). "But in these forms is expressed the equilibrium of severity and mercy. Mercy being masculine and severity feminine. Excess of Mercy is merely weakness, but Excess of Severity calls forth the evil and oppressive force which is symbolised by Leviathan. Wherefore it is said 'Behind the shoulders of the Bride, the Serpent rears his head.' Of the Bride" (the cow-headed Isis) "not the Supernal Mother" (Isis crowned with the Royal diadem) "for she bruises the head of the Serpent."

The serpent is the centripetal force, ever seeking to penetrate paradise, and "thereby constricting the efflux of divine radiation," which is centrifugal. The Adam Qadmon's exchange of the Garden of Eden for knowledge and death, must be taken to mean the exchange of uncreated thought into differentiation and evolution, resulting finally in the creation of a material universe.

On this subject much may be learnt from the first book of the *Divine Pymander*, published in this series;[3] in the Seventeenth book it is written:—

> "Moreover the things that are made are visible, but *He is invisible;* and for *this cause he maketh them*, that *he may be visible;* and therefore he maketh them always."

So we see that the Eternal one being defined, saw a reflection of himself; and the love he bore his image emanated as a third form, the Supernal Mother who aspireth to the Wisdom which is beyond. So is the Supernal triad formed.

In like manner the Holy Triad, reflected and defined, became the throne whereon the holy deific form was seated, and the Hexagram of the Macroprosopus was reflected unto the Heart of the Microprosopus.

And in this sense are to be understood the words written on the mummy case of Panehemisis, "The heart of Man is his own God."

Around the image in the sanctuary of our hearts is the firmament and the powers, and below are the Kerubim or Living Creatures.

In his book entitled *Lumen de Lumine*, our author laments the separation that has taken place between the Elemental, Celestial, and Spiritual Sciences, for he says, these three are branches of one tree.

"Out of one universal root, the Chaos, grew all specified natures and their individuals."

I must deal shortly with the nature of Chaos as understood by the ancients, because in the present volume our author evades any definite explanation of it.

Chaos, the Abyss or "Great Deep" was personified among the Egyptians by Neith; the only one containing all—without form or sex, giving birth to itself without fecundation. She was adored under the form of a Virgin Mother. She is the Father-Mother, the immaculate Virgin. She is called the Lady of the Sycamore, and is represented as dispersing the waters of the Tree of Life. She is the Bythos of the Gnostics, The One of the Neoplatonists, The All of the German Metaphysicians, the Anaita of Assyria.

Now from this root or chaos sprang all manifestations, divine, celestial, and elemental, and these three are one, and if separated from each other are like the dead branches cut from the parent stem.

For some pages our author dwells on the exoteric meaning of the scriptures in a manner that concerns the modern thinker very little. But we must bear in memory the intolerance and bigotry that prevailed at the period, and that twenty years later Spinoza forfeited all worldly advantages by asserting that the vulgar interpretation of the Sacred Oracles had led to much error.

However, Thomas Vaughan having paid his tribute to "weak consciences," touches us all when he says, "God minds the Restitution of Nature in general, and not of Man alone, ... who is but a small part of nature. Regeneration, Illumination and Grace, signify a new influence of Spirit. If God and Nature be one, how much more shall man and nature be one."

Emerson has said in this relation, "Indeed we are but Shadows we are not endowed with real life and all that seems most real about us is but the thinnest substance of a dream, till the heart be touched by nature. That touch creates us: then we begin to be; thereby we are beings of reality and inheritors of eternity."

We acknowledge nature to be corrupt, but by the knowledge of that corruption is to be solved the riddle of the Universe.

The union of spirit and nature gives rise to a perfect compound. The Light of wisdom united by philosophy to experiment makes the perfect artist or creative adept.

Philosophy or the passion for wisdom stimulates the intellect, as religion stimulates the emotions: these passions or expansions of the Ego carry it beyond the limits of its own being, and tend to merge it in the all being. Here the centrifugal or redeeming force is free to act, and the constrictions of matter cease. When the Passions of the Emotions and the Intellect are set free, the Experience of Elemental Nature can be judged with safety. This then is the Esoteric meaning of the "Unity with God." "I am in my father, and ye in me, and I in you." (St. John x. 14-20.) Compare again, "His is the mind, theirs are the powers" of the *Chaldæan Oracles*. For the perfect man stands between the finest ether and the coarsest matter, and his spirit must penetrate all.

For the world, religion means, as Cardinal Newman puts it, "the knowledge of God, of His will, and of our duties towards Him." Separating Him as a formal notion from His works, cutting Him off as a branch from the Tree of Life of which He is the very root and being. Therefore to the initiated it is no blasphemy to say that such religion is a vanity and vexation of spirit.

The world holds many half evolved personalities who have to live and learn much before they can be conscious of the latent complexities of their own natures. Their hour has not yet come. But for the more fully developed,—life daily sounds undreamed of harmonies. Just as in modern music the most acute emotion is produced by subtle changes of key, so the human being in passing from one aspect to another of a highly complex existence intensifies and enriches his being with experiences, undreamed of by the undeveloped man, just as little as, by the masters of the simple harmonies of ancient music.

Our author's first paragraph ends with the clear statement that without philosophy, or the passion for wisdom, salvation cannot be understood. Again he pleads for the union of the divine, the celestial, and the natural; for he says the very nature of the highest existence is the union and synthesis of the diverse products of differentiation.

Can we not dimly comprehend from this principle how it is that each day of Brahma (or manifestation of the Universe) enriches and beautifies the night of his repose; how Nirvana becomes more and more exquisite in its subtle harmonies, as beings are prepared for it by finer and finer complexities and variations of parts.

COMMENTS UPON THE SECOND PARAGRAPH.

This is a recapitulation of the general principle that God and Nature,—Scripture and Philosophy—are to be joined together and not separated from each other in our minds.

COMMENTS UPON THE FIFTH PARAGRAPH.

Thomas Vaughan begins by defining the creative deity as the formulator and manifestor of the visible world. He pictures him as an artificer working upon pre-existent substance. As I have already pointed out, this idea is that of the Jehovah of the Jews in relation to the Ehyeh and Ain Soph Aur. This latter principle must, however, be regarded by us at present as the Divine Neith or Chaos, also explained in the notes on the first paragraph. This fundamental virgin substance is only to be understood, says Vaughan, by the study of seeds.

Now if we cut open any moderate-sized seed, we shall find an outer covering, two masses of starchy matter, and a root or radicle.

In the root we have the image of the One from whom spring the many; in the two halves the positive and negative nourishing or preserving principles; and in the coat or cover the constricting force without which manifest form is impossible, but which must be overcome for growth to take place.

The seed planted in the ground becomes a sugary fœculent mass, and in the midst of putrefaction and fermentation the new living being grows and becomes manifest. The study of embryology takes us a long way towards the solution of the mystery of life. We start with the protyle or protoplasm of modern science, we trace the beginnings of a human being through stages akin to the mollusc, the fish, the reptile, and the monkey. This protyle or secondary chaos, which so much resembles the Hyle or sediment of the waters of creation is most evident to the unscientific mind in the scum of a stagnant pool.

M. Pasteur has shewn us that the air is full of microscopic life, that it can be found everywhere, from the bloom of a peach to the liver of a pig; that it can be taken thence and made to germinate in any gelatine, syrup, or glycerine basis; that the white corpuscles of blood are minute living organisms, capable of being oxygenated, and that they, like gold, become red in the process. This is no doubt a materialistic translation of our author›s meaning; but the evolution of the highest is similar to the evolution of the lowest, as is taught us by the *Emerald Tablet* of Hermes.

All my researches lead me to consider that the great mystery of the origin of life consists almost entirely of a measure of temperature. Life is *latent* everywhere; it merely awaits the time in the cooling of a world that is appropriate to its manifestation. Let us at the same time bear in mind the Kabbalistic and mystical interpretation of the "Foundation," and its connection with the emanations of the microcosm.

COMMENTS UPON THE SIXTH PARAGRAPH.

This calls attention to the fact that difference of circumstance alone congeals the prima materia into metals, vegetables, or animals. We know very well that between the lowest forms of animal and vegetable life, between the small water fungi and the hydra or amœba there is very little to choose; in fact, if we look upon the brain of an animal as corresponding to the root of a tree, we shall find extraordinary similarities even in the more complex developments of the two great kingdoms. Minerals, on the other hand, are created and formulated at such high temperatures, and are so much more durable that it is not at once obvious to us that the principle of evolution is the same.

The Arabians called the prima materia, "Halicali," from Hali-summum, and Calop—bonum; but the Latin Authors corruptly write it Sal Alkali. This Summum Bonum is the Catholic receptacle of spirits, it is blessed and impregnated with Light from above, and was therefore styled by Magicians—Domus Signata, plena Luminis Divinitatis.[4]

COMMENTS UPON THE SEVENTH PARAGRAPH.

Here we find our author distinctly associates his Chaos with that which is behind Kether—the first emanation of Deity; God with Chokmah or the Abba of the Kabbalists; Nature with Binah or the Aima or Mother, the third emanation. Or we may put it thus; from the Chaos or Neith sprang God or the Father, and

Nature or the Mother; from their union sprang the secondary Chaos or first reflected triangle. Thus completing the Hexad of the Macrocosm.

COMMENTS UPON THE NINTH PARAGRAPH.

Our author calls the elements, Earth. Water, Air, and Heaven or Fiery Water.

From these by digestion and sublimation the gases, vapours, and clouds are derived. This is what in ordinary occult language is called the firmament, the Yetziratic or formative world.

From this is distilled a clear water of the nature of wine or alcohol.

By congelation is obtained a fiery sulphurons substance as wine becomes acid vinegar by exposure to a certain heat, this acetate will run into an oily burning gum or glass when duly concentrated.

Vitriol vapour and liquid sulphur are not dealt with in this volume.

I will now supply a scale of attribution and analogies between the Macrocosm and the Microcosm.

The sun and moon are allotted by Cornelius Agrippa to the eyes, as being the lights of the greater and lesser worlds.

The other planets to the nostrils, mouth, and ears.

These, then, typify the parts of the Spiritual Consciousness or divine in man.

The lungs are the seat of the firmament, and in them circulates the air we breathe.

The heart, the central fire, the Archæus. The blood with its constant pulse, the sea full of sulphurous volatile fatness.

Our author next points out that the interior heat is greatest when the light is latent.

He then says clearly that Pure Earth is Nitre, better known to us as saltpetre—a white powder which attracts moisture, and by eliminating the mineral potash forms nitric acid, one of the most corrosive acids that we have. (Of course I need not point out that another proportion of oxygen and nitrogen gives us the ordinary air we breathe. He then shows that the latent heat contained in snow will, if hermetically sealed, cause a glass to break more rapidly than the latent heat in ordinary water.

COMMENTS UPON THE TENTH PARAGRAPH.

The sap restrained by the cold of winter doubtless accumulates force proportionate to the strength of its prison walls. Like an arrow released it flies further, according to the weight of the bow which propels it.

COMMENTS UPON THE ELEVENTH PARAGRAPH.

Vaughan here returns to Mr. Rice, of Chester, or Rhæsus Cestrensis, whose Latin aphorism was quoted in the third paragraph, and deals with the meaning of the word elementates or secondary elements, which are generated in the same manner as simple elements by the application of a gentle heat and moisture.

Then our author is reminded of the association of the reincarnating ego with the os coccygis[5] by the Jews; after a lengthy digression on this subject, he hints that particular minerals are to be regenerated in the same way as universal elements; we presume he wishes to point out that in the same way as simple life is generated, so a complex being can also be regenerated.

It is worthy of note that phosphorus discovered by Brand in 1669, is prepared from bones, and has many properties in common with the secret fire of the Alchemists.

COMMENTS UPON THE TWELFTH PARAGRAPH.

Vaughan points out that the vapours of the sea are bituminous, saltish, mercurial, moist and phlegmatic. The exhalations of the earth are hot and mineral, nitrous, arsenical, sulphurous; and in the air all these things are mixed together and resolved.

He then points out that salts tend to liquefy if left in moist air. That quicksilver volatilizes, and on being divided into minute particles loses its identity in the atmosphere; but it is to be presumed that it merely turns into an oxide of mercury and falls to the earth, as many other matters do under the corrosive influence of oxygen.

COMMENTS UPON THE THIRTEENTH PARAGRAPH.

The action of Fire tends to overcome what we call the gravitation of matter. The action of air is to transmute or oxgyenize matter. To congeal and coagulate gravitation and magnetism must be brought to bear on the substance.

COMMENTS UPON THE FOURTEENTH PARAGRAPH.

Study, search, think, and experiment for yourselves. So only can you find the light that will make your particular life a living reality. To accept a ready-made belief blindly is to commit mental and moral suicide. You must slay the delusions, the constrictive forces by which you find yourself surrounded when you start on your search for light. You must fight and conquer the dragons of habit and custom which stultify your spiritual consciousness; kill them and wash yourself in their blood, like the heroes of old. You must fail, and fall, and then rise again; you must strip yourself of all idolatrous shams, until you find the vivifying idea or light which shall render your life fruitful. Each man or woman must do this for him or herself. This is the teaching of the Brothers of the Rosy Cross, and it is the only living truth, for it has no finality; and the Nemesis of all reformers is finality.

But this truth has never more than half dawned upon the world; the leader of each wave of evolution looks upon those who went before him as having erred. But the Heroic Man is always right for the time he lives in. Dante was right in the age when Catholicism was a living force; Shakespeare was right when feudalism was a living force. So Luther was right when only the husk of a religion was left, and Cromwell was in the right when the belief in the divine right of kings had died out in his race.

When we have found the constructive faith that has the inherent force to carry us onwards, we shall be right. But what that is, only the heart of each man can tell him.

In the midst of the Renaissance, through the Reformation, and Civil Wars. and after the narrowing fights of the schoolmen. Bacon called on all men to weigh and consider for themselves.

Vaughan was echoing this cry when he hurled abuse at the critic and exalted the artist and craftsman, for Aristotle must ever be the type of the former, as Plato is the type of the latter.

But we must not forget in reading the works of Vaughan, that the dawn of experimental science had scarcely appeared when they were written. For much that is a commonplace to us, would have been considered a miracle at that time; and we must appreciate the vigour of his intellect when we find him saying so much in 1655 that is still being said by those who have thought out for themselves a complete theory of life based upon a clear knowledge of its possibilities and its limitations. Not a little of Vaughan's wisdom might be well accepted by those who study the metaphysical side of life; but who disdain to put in practice any of the theories they are so busy in promulgating.

For, as he says, "without effect, Philosophy is useless and not to be numbered among our necessities."

COMMENTS UPON THE SEVENTEENTH PARAGRAPH.

By earth our author understands nitre, salt-petre, *etc.* It may be suggestive to point out that in all alchemical receipts we find nitre and sea-salt (symbolised by a circle divided by a vertical or a horizontal line respectively), as the two essential constituents of the *materia magica*. And that aqua regia or the acid which alone can resolve gold, is made of a mixture of nitric and hydrochloric acids.

The Solar Oriental Earth is probably orpiment or some mixture of antimony, for although pure antimony is of little use in transmutation there is no doubt that it contains, under certain conditions, native properties not to be found in other substances.

COMMENTS UPON THE EIGHTEENTH PARAGRAPH.

The whole of this paragraph is worthy of the most attentive study, and may be interpreted on all planes, with advantage to the student of occultism. Taking for instance the

	Natural.	Philosophical.	Religious
Passion (expansion)	Fire	The flash of an idea	Enthusiasm,impulse
Intuition (instinct)	Water	Creative imagination (Nourishing the idea)	Aspiration
Vehicle (the medium)	Air	Formulative intelligence (The word)	Emotional energy
The nourisher (the manifestor)	Earth	The completed work	Complete commun- ion

The three alchemical principles may be taken as the principles of centrifugal, centripetal and circulatory motion; or as corroding, penetrating, and preserving, according to the commonly understood characteristics of sulphur, mercury and salt.

COMMENTS UPON THE TWENTIETH PARAGRAPH.

Deals with the nature of philosophical fire, that it is moist and invisible as the heat of a hot-bed or forcing-house; or a humid, tepid fire, blood warm.

There are different degrees of heat for the black, white, and red stages of the work, but the first must be gentle and moist. Here again we have the symbolism of thought and gentle melancholy, purity, and finally practical power.

COMMENTS UPON THE TWENTY-FIRST PARAGRAPH.

Deals with the putrefying agent as a centrifugal energy, for until the elements have fallen out among themselves the celestial influence cannot descend.

Until we are conscious of our present imperfections, we cannot receive the perfecting influence.

Comments upon the Twenty-Second Paragraph.

It is not the vehicle that coagulates, but the matter borne in the vehicle. Here it will be well to remember the Kabbalistic definitions of the parts of the Soul. The Earth or The Nephesh is the aura or lower astral. The Water or The Neshamah is the throne of the spirit. The Fire or The Chiah, and Neshamah form the Wheels and the Throne of the Incarnating Ego (Yechidah) or the real spirit of the Triple Fire. While the air, or the human Ego, is the meeting place of the other forces.

Comments upon the Twenty-Fifth Paragraph.

But the gum or jelly of water feeds all things. Manna is a translation of the Hebrew word Man, meaning occultly the mixture of the upper and lower waters; the waters of creation in the chariot of the waters of the floods.

The fire that was hid in the pit, the fire of the altar, may, of course, have been any inflammable spirit or oil, such as spirits of wine, petroleum or a preparation of phosphorus, limelight or even an application of electrical force. But there is a deeper meaning to be looked for in the passage quoted from Maccabees.

This paragraph ends with an apology for the Jews, whom, it must remembered, were at this time, still looked upon with loathing by the Christians.

Comments upon the Twenty-Sixth Paragraph.

We now come to the connecting link between the parts of this volume. We have here a series of actual quotations from the *Emerald Tablet* of Chiram Trismegistus, or as he is commonly called, Hermes.

Of the four luminaries I may here quote a passage from our author's book called *Lumen de Lumine*.

"'It is most certain that no Astrabolism takes place without some grievous corruption and alteration in the Patient, for Nature works not but in loose moyst discomposed Elements. When the Elements fall out among themselves, the Celestial Fire reconciles them and generates some new Form, seeing the old one could consist no longer. ... The body must be reduced to sperm, which receives the Impress of the Stars, and must immediately be exposed to the fire of Nature.' ... When she had thus said she took out two Miraculous Medals. I did not conceive there was in Nature such glorious substances, she called them the Saphirics of the Sun and Moon."

The sun and the moon are the Cœlestial luminaries, but the central ones are a fire hidden in the earth or nitre, and an airy lunar nature in the water.

These two mixed natures are known to us as the desires of the flesh and the phantasies of the imagination: in their transmutation by consecration of the desires and purification of the thoughts, lies the pathway to wisdom.

The will and the imagination of an adept are symbolised by the Urim and Thummim of the High Priest; with this key read the paragraph carefully, and it will give you food for much profitable reflection.

COMMENTS UPON THE TWENTY-SEVENTH PARAGRAPH.

This points out that the only means of multiplying metallic natures is to apply their sulphurous nature to the universal feminine fat water; the oxide or tincture of a metal if dealt with according to art with a careful adjustment of temperature, may then be treated as a ferment.

But as I have said from the beginning, the author is too vague for ns to derive any clue to practical alchemy from his work, and I will content myself by pointing out that the human passions, Pride, Envy, Anger, Sloth, Avarice, Gluttony, Lust, have long been associated with the seven gross metals, and that the oxidised metals may be regarded as symbolic of their saving virtues, Humility, Love, Patience, Fortitude, Compassion, Temperance and Chastity.

The Union of a particular to a universal exalts and multiplies strongly. Here is the final lesson then. Let us recognise that only the merging of our human wills with the Universal Will can result in hastening the day of our perfection. It we labour against the World's Will we shall fail, and our work will vanish from off the face of the earth.

COMMENTS UPON THE APPENDIX.

I will end as I began by saying, I have read many Alchemical Treatises, but never one of less use to the practical Alchemist, than this. At the same time I have come across few occult works that have helped me more in my search for the secrets of these Great Adepts—who are the Masters of our Race.

S.S.D.D.

"Alas, Alas, that all men should possess the Master-soul, be one with the World-soul, and that possessing it, the Master-soul should so little avail them."
The Book of Golden Precepts.

finis.

Notes:
1. Reprinted from *Euphrates; or, The Waters of the East* by Eugenius Philalethes. Collectanea Hermetica Vol. VII. London: Theosophical Publishing Society, 1896.—D.K.
2. The actual quote from *The Chaldæan Oracles of Zoroaster*, is "16. Power is with them, but Mind is front Him." Proclus in *Platonis Theologiam*, 365. T.—D.K.
3. See *The Divine Pymander of Hermes*. Collectanea Hermetica Vol. II. Golden Dawn Research Trust, 2011.—D.K.
4. The "Domus Signata, plena Luminis Divinitatis" is Latin for "The house is sealed and filled with Divine Light."—D.K.

5. The Latin term coccyx or coccyges (plural) is commonly referred to as the tailbone of a human. The word originally comes from the Greek κόκκυξ which means "cuckoo", and refers to the curved shape of the bird›s beak when viewed from the side.—D.K.

A Collection of Information on Colour: Part I[1]

R.R. et A.C. Colour Scheme
(Source Unknown)

TheFive Elements in the Four [Colour] Scales
of King, Queen, Prince and Princess.

Spirit (⊕) as an Element.

King: White merging into grey.
Sigil of Spirit in King Scale:

Queen: Deep purple merging into black.
Sigil of Spirit in Queen Scale:

Prince: 7 Rainbow colours with purple outermost.
Sigil of Spirit in Prince Scale:

Princess: 5 colours: white, red, yellow, black and blue outermost.
Sigil of Spirit in Princess Scale:

Fire (△) as an Element.

King: Glowing orange scarlet.
Sigil of Fire in King Scale:

Queen: Vermillian red.
Sigil of Fire in Queen Scale:

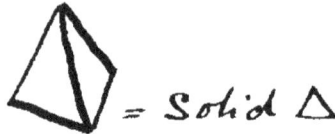

= Solid △

Prince: Scarlet red flecked with yellow. (*Nota bene*: flecks can be appropriate Hebrew letter י's.)
Sigil of Fire in Prince Scale:

Princess: Vermillian flecked with crimson and emerald green.
Flash pink. (Flecks can be appropriate Hebrew letter ה's.)
Sigil of Fire in Princess Scale:

Water (▽) as an Element.

King: Deep blue.
Sigil of Water in King Scale:

Queen: White and dull sapphire green.
Sigil of Water in Queen Scale:

Prince: Deep olive green.
Sigil of Water in Prince Scale:

Princess: White flecked with purple; a glow like mother of pearl.
Sigil of Water in Princess Scale:

Air (△) as an Element.

King: Bright pale yellow.
Sigil of Air in King Scale:

Queen: Sky blue.
Sigil of Air in Queen Scale:

Prince: Blue green.
Sigil of Air in Prince Scale:

Princess: Emerld with golden flecks; whirl in centre.
Sigil of Air in Princess Scale:

Earth (▽) as an Element.

King: Black and 3 tertiaries: [citrine, olive and russet].
Sigil of Earth in King Scale:

Queen: Amber yellow.
Sigil of Earth in Queen Scale:

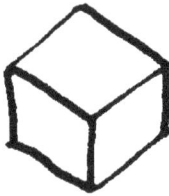

Solid cube

Prince: Dark brown.
Sigil of Earth in Prince Scale:

Princess: Black flecked with yellow.
Sigil of Earth in Princess Scale:

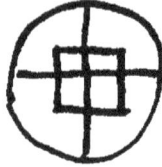

The Sephiroth in the 4 Scales of King, Queen, Prince and Princess.

	King	Queen	Prince	Princess
כ	Uncoloured brilliance.	White brilliance.	White brilliance.	White rayed with golden.
ח	Pure soft blue.	Grey.	Blue pearl grey mother of pearl.	White flecked with red, blue and yellow.
ב	Crimison.	Black.	Black and crimson = dull dark brown.	Grey flecked with pink.
ה	Deep violet.	Blue.	Deep purple.	Deep orange flecked with yellow.
ג	Orange.	Scarlet red.	Bright scarlet.	Red flecked with black.
ת	Clear rose pink.	Yellow.	Rich salmon.	Golden amber.
נ	Amber.	Emerald green.	Bright yellow green.	Olive flecked with golden.
ה	Violet purple.	Orange.	Red russet.	Yellow brown flecked with white.
י	Indigo.	Violet.	Very dark purple.	Citrine flecked with azure.
מ	Yellow.	4 tertiary colours.[1]	Tertiaries flecked with glowing gold.	Black rayed with yellow.

The Planets in the 4 Scales of King, Queen, Prince and Princess.

	King	Queen	Prince	Princess
♄	Indigo.	Black.	Blue black.	Black rayed with blue.
♃	Violet.	Blue.	Rich purple.	Bright blue rayed with yellow.
♂	Scarlet.	Red.	Flame scarlet.	Scarlet rayed with amber.
☉	Orange.	Golden yellow.	Rich amber.	Amber rayed with red.
♀	Emerald.	Sky blue.	Spring green.	Cerise rayed with pale green.
☿	Yellow.	Purple.	Grey.	Indigo rayed with violet.
☽	Blue.	Silvery white.	Very cold pale blue.	Silver rayed with sky blue.

The Zodiac in the 4 Scales of King, Queen, Prince and Princess.

	King	Queen	Prince	Princess
♈	Scarlet.	Red.	Brilliant flame.	Glowing red.
♉	Deep orange.	Deep indigo.	Deep warm	Rich brown. olive.
♊	Orange.	Pale mauve.	Colour of new leather.	Reddish grey inclined to mauve.
♋	Amber.	Deep brown maroon.	Rich bright russet brown.	Dark greenish brown.
♌	Greenish yellow.	Deep purple.	Grey.	Reddish amber.
♍	Yellow green.	Slate grey.	Green grey.	Violet or plum colour.
♎	Emerald.	Blue.	Deep blue green.	Light pale green.
♏	Greenish blue.	Dull brown.	Very dark brown.	Vivid indigo brown like the back of a live lobster.
♐	Blue.	Yellow.	Green.	Dark vivid blue.

♑	Indigo.	Black.	Blue black.	Cold dark grey, nearly black.
♒	Violet.	Sky blue.	Bluish mauve.	White tinged with purple.
♓	Crimison.	Buff flecked with glistering silvery white.	Light translucent	Stone colour. brown of a pinkish tinge.

[The colour of the 3 Alchemical Symbols.]

[Sulphur: Pale red or] pink.

[Salt:] Pale blue.

[Mercury:] Pale yellow.

End of R.R. et A.C. information.

Notes:
1. The material here is from the Notebooks of S.S.D.D.–D.K.
2. R.R. et A.C. are initials for the Latin phrase Rosæ Rubeæ et Aureæ Crucis.–D.K.
3. The four tertiary colours are: citrine, olive, russet and black.– D.K.

A Collection of Information on Colour: Part II

The Four Colour Scales
(Based on Hodos Chamelionis)

There are four scales of colour which correspond to the Four Kabbalistic Worlds. They are:

Scales	Worlds	Tarot Suits	Tetragrammaton	Elements
King	Atziluth	Wands	י (Yod)	△ (Fire)
Queen	Briah	Cups	ה (He)	▽ (Water)
Prince	Yetzirah	Swords	ו (Vau)	△ (Air)
Princess	Assiah	Pentacles	ה (He)	▽ (Earth)

The following tables consists of a classification of the scales of colour in each of the Four Kabbalistic Worlds. The first ten refer to the Sephiroth and the remaining twenty-two refer to the Paths.

	King Scale	Queen Scale	Prince Scale	Princess Scale
1:	Uncoloured brillance.	White brillance.	White brillance.	White rayed golden.
2:	Pure soft blue.	Grey.	Blue pearl grey, mother of pearl.	White flecked red, blue and yellow.
3:	Crimson.	Black with hidden red.	Black and crimison = dull dark brown.	Grey flecked pink.
4:	Deep violet.	Blue.	Deep purple.	Deep orange flecked yellow.
5:	Orange.	Scarlet red.	Bright scarlet.	Red flecked black.
6:	Clear rose pink.	Yellow (gold).	Rich salmon.	Golden amber.
7:	Amber.	Emerald green.	Bright yellow green.	Olive flecked golden.
8:	Violet purple.	Orange.	Red russet.	Yellow brown flecked white.
9:	Indigo.	Violet.	Very dark purple.	Citrine flecked azure.
10:	Yellow.	Citrine, olive, russet, black.	4 tertiaries flecked glowing gold.	Black rayed yellow.

King Scale	Queen Scale	Prince Scale	Princess Scale
11: Bright pale yellow.	Sky blue.	Blue green.	Emerald green flecked golden.
12: Yellow.	Purple.	Grey.	Indigo rayed violet.
13: Blue.	Silvery white.	Very cold pale blue.	Silver rayed sky blue.
14: Emerald green.	Sky blue.	Early spring green.	Cerise rayed pale green.
15: Scarlet.	Red.	Brilliant flame.	Glowing red.
16: Deep orange.	Deep indigo.	Deep warm olive.	Rich brown.
17: Orange.	Pale mauve.	Colour of new leather. [Yellow pale brown.]	Reddish grey inclined to mauve.
18: Amber.	Deep brown maroon.	Rich bright russet brown.	Dark greenish brown.
19: Green yellow.	Deep purple.	Grey.	Reddish amber.
20: Yellow green.	Slate grey.	Green grey.	Violet or plum colour.
21: Violet.	Blue.	Rich purple.	Bright blue rayed yellow.
22: Emerald green.	Blue.	Deep blue green.	Light pale green.
23: Deep blue.	White and dull sapphire green.	Deep olive green.	White flecked purple like mother of pearl.
24: Greenish blue.	Dull brown.	Very dark brown.	Vivid indigo brown like back of lobster.
25: Blue	Yellow.	Green.	Dark vivid blue.
26: Indigo.	Black.	Blue black.	Cold dark grey, near black.
27: Scarlet.	Red.	Flame scarlet.	Scarlet rayed amber.
28: Violet.	Sky blue.	Bluish mauve.	White tinged purple.
29: Crimson.	Buff flecked silvery white.	Light translucent brown with pink.	Stone colour.
30: Orange.	Golden yellow.	Rich amber.	Amber rayed red.
31: Glowing orange scarlet.	Vermillion red.	Scarlet red flecked yellow.	Vermillion flecked crimson and emerald.
31: Indigo.	Black.	Blue black.	Black rayed blue.
32: Black, citrine, olive, russet.	Amber yellow.	Dark brown.	Black flecked yellow.
32: White merging grey.	Deep purple merging black.	7 rainbow colours (purple outside).	White, red, yellow, black, blue (outside).
Daäth:			
Lavender.	Grey white.	Pure violet.	Grey flecked gold.

A Collection of Information on Colour: Part III

Of Flashing Sounds[1]

From the Note Book of Iehi Aour

The Zodiac in the Chromatic Scale.

Sign		Scale	Colour
♈	Aries.	C.	Red.
♉	Taurus.	C#.	Red-orange.
♊	Gemini.	D.	Orange.
♋	Cancer.	D#.	Amber [orange-yellow].
♌	Leo.	E.	Yellow.
♍	Virgo.	F.	Green-yellow.
♎	Libra.	F#.	Green.
♏	Scorpio.	G.	Blue-green.
♐	Sagittarius.	G#.	Blue.
♑	Capricorn.	A.	Indigo [blue-violet].
♒	Aquarius.	A#.	Violet.
♓	Pisces.	B.	Magenta [violet-red].

The Mother Letters [with the new Planets].

Letter	[Planet]	Scale	Colour	Sounds	Flash on
ש Shin.	[ף Pluto.]	C.	Red.	F#.	Green.
א Aleph.	[♅ Uranus.]	E.	Yellow.	A#.	Violet.
מ Mem.	[♆ Neptune.]	G#.	Blue.	D.	Orange.

Fundamental Notes of the Planets.

Planet	Scale	Colour	Planet	Sounds	Flash on
♂ Mars.	C.	Red.	Venus.	F#.	Green.
☉ Sun.	D.	Orange.	Moon.	G#.	Blue.
☿ Mercury.	E.	Yellow.	Jupiter.	A#.	Violet.
♀ Venus.	F#.	Green.	Mars.	C.	Red.
☽ Moon.	G#.	Blue.	Sun.	D.	Orange.
♃ Jupiter.	A#.	Violet.	Venus.	E.	Yellow.
[♄ Saturn.	A.	Indigo.		F.	Green-yellow.]

Notes:
1. These notes are by Allan Bennett (*Iehi Aour*) of his research he did on colour and sound scales based upon the Hebrew Alphabet (Twelve Zodiac, the three Mother letters and the seven Planets). Interestingly, these are the same associations that Paul Foster Case used in his writings.—D.K.
2. Aleister Crowley has written a query in Bennett's Notebook: "B = Saturn?"—D.K.

A Collection of Information on Colour: Part IV

Additional Notes On Colour

By Sapientia Sapienti Dono Data

ACCORDING to H.P. Blavatsky the 7 colours of the rainbow were arranged in vibration bearing the same relation to each other, *viz*:−

$$1, 2, 3, 4, 5, 6, 7.$$

As the overtones or harmonics of a fundamental note. You will find in *Ganot's Physics*[1] the statements that overtones are most readily detected in brass musical instruments; and also that overtones beyond the 7th are nasal and unpleasant in sound. The overtones for the fundamental note F would be:

Octaves each contain twice the number of vibrations of the one below it. As for example: 2, 4, 8, 16, 32, and is forth hence; red, orange, green and the ghostly chemical ray stand in the relation of octaves to each other.

This is my own working out of the information given to me with regard to H.P.B's Esoteric teaching to be found in scientific text books. So that all the Occult information contained in it comes from a Hindu source.

Signed Sapientia
May 1900.

From an Occult Persian source I learn that colours, sounds and motions as used in Oriental dancing have the following emotional effects:

Coral red: The splendour and tragedy of Life.

Orange: The dance of destiny. Blare of Trumpets. The overwhelming circumstance of Life.

Topaz yellow: Loud rejoicing, blatant cries and leaping in the air.

Emerald green: Wisdom of the Ancient Babylonians. The dance is done with gestures of the arms and body by kneeling figures and the mind turns to curious mysteries.

Sapphire: The conquering element of Beethoven's music comes with this tremendously forceful colour. Victorious in love or hate.

Ruby: It must reach into the palest Amethyst when it becomes the most Occult and wonderful of colours.

The four Queens may be considered analagous in colours to:

[Queen of Pentacles] - *Pale amber*: Giving the emotion which creates works of art.

[Queen of Swords] - *Clear pale blue*: Gives Clairvoyance and subtle apprehension.

[Queen of Cups] - *Eau de Mil* [Water of thousands (white and dull sapphire green)]: Pity and tenderness needs to be fused with the next.

[Queen of Wands] - *Pale green fire* [or vermillion red]: Swiftness and fiery rhythmic motion. This is the force that animates reformers. (*Green* and *red* are said in Volume III of *The Secret Doctrine* to be occulty and interchangeable as the Lower Manas and Karma alternately can occupy the same vehicle.)

Earth: [No diagram added. □ ?]

Air: [No diagram added. ○ ?]

Water: [No diagram added. ⌒ ?]

Fire: [No diagram added. △ ?]

These may be combined with the following shapes and be formed to correspond to the 4 Hindu Tatwas.[2]

There is also an Ancient Arab method of making circles and other forms in fire round an operator. It was performed on the desert near the sea shore.

A square [Earth]: For knowledge of construction and building.

A circular fire [Air]: It was used to gain knowledge of the revolution of the stars.

A semi-circle [Water]: For knowledge of healing and physiology and herbs.

A triangle [Fire]: For the knowledge of metals and things under the earth.

Pale amber [square]: Art and construction of buildings.

Clear pale blue circle: Giving subtle apprehension of the Stars. Sky.

Eau de Mil [Water of thousands] semi-circle: Pity and healing by herbs.

Pale green fire [triangle]: Fierce motion of the breaking open of the mineral world.

This is interesting because it comes from quite independent sources.

Notes:
1. *Ganot's Physics: experimental and applied for the use of college and school.* Translated by E. Atkinson. Rairaido, 1895. —D.K.
2. The Hindu Tatwas consist of:— Akasha - Spirit - Black or Indigo Vesica Piscis: $\bigcirc$. Prithivi - Earth - Yellow Square: $\square$. Vayu - Air - Sky Blue Circle: $\bigcirc$. Apas - Water - Silver or White Crescent: $\smile$. Tejas - Fire - Red Triangle: $\triangle$.—D.K.

The Workings of Farr's Sphere Group

[On 17 January 1901, Florence Farr issued a "semi-official statement" of the magical workings of the Sphere Group to Second Order members of the Rosæ Rubeæ et Aureæ Crucis. This was the response to Annie Horniman's (Fortiter et Recte) critical petition against the Sphere Group which was given to the Chiefs of the Second Order. She wrote that the "group consisted of 12 members and the symbols were adapted from the Star maps and Tree of Life projected on a sphere, whence they were sometimes called the Sphere Croup. The twelve members had astral stations assigned to them around this sphere and a certain Egyptian astral form was supposed to occupy the centre." (Ellic Howe, *The Magicans of the Golden Dawn*, (1972) p. 247.) The first incarnation of the Sphere Group (No. 1) used the figure of an Egyptian Adept in the centre of the Sphere, but was later changed to an image of the Holy Grail in the second incarnation of the Group.

In R.W. Felkin's paper called "The Group as I knew it, and Fortiter [Horniman]" he wrote that the objects of the Sphere Group "were: to concentrate forces of growth, progress and purification, every Sunday at noon, and the progress was 1st, the formation of the twelve workers near but not in 36 [Blythe Road]; 2nd Formulation round London; 3rd, Formulation round the Earth; 4th, Formulation among the Constellations. Then gradually reverse the process, bringing the quintessence of the greater forces to the lesser. The process was to take about an hour." (Howe, (1972) p. 250.)

Robert Turner described the Workings of the Sphere Group as a group which "consisted of twelve members [who] each held to represent an individual Zodiacal potency—it seems likely that an unmentioned thirteenth member acted as Seer. During the Sphere ceremonies (which took place every Sunday at noon), the Adepti positioned themselves at equal distances around an Astrally constructed spherical image and invoked the presence of an Egyptian Spirit-form which manifested at the exact centre of their magical structure. As the ceremony progressed the 'Sphere' was gradually expanded (Astrally) until by degrees it encompassed: the place of Working, the City of London, the Earth, and finally the entire Solar System. After the required Astral communication had been received at a Super-Celestial level the 'Sphere' was caused to slowly contract, in an effort to draw the power back to the Earth Plane." ('The Sphere Workings: The Enochian Alphabet Clairvoyantly Examined' in *The Monolith*, Vol. II, No. 2, (1977), p. 17.) —D.K.]

The Working of Sphere Group (No. 1)[1]

87 the Grove Hammersmith W.
17 January, 1901

Care V.H. Fra[ter] Sub Spe,[2]
It seems necessary for me to make a semi-official statement to the Theorici regarding my work in the Order during the last 3 years in order to account for the present state of feeling of which naturally you became aware on your visit to London.

You may remember at the end of the year 1895 I came across an Egyptian Adept in the British Museum and freely told other members of the possibilities opened out. On Jan. 27th 1896 I received a long letter from D.D.C.F.[3] in reply to a letter of mine sending a charged drawing of the Egyptian and asking him if I were not grossly deceived by her claiming to be equal in rank to an 8°=3° of our Order at the same time giving me numbers which I afterwards calculated to be correct for that grade. I still possess his letter approving altogether of my working with her, and saying it was necessary to make offerings & then all would be well—*&c. &c.* I soon found there was a considerable prejudice against Egyptian Symbolism amongst the members of the Order and I began to hold my tongue after having recommended the various clearly marked groups of

thinkers (such as Indian, Christian and so on) to work steadily
and regularly by themselves each under some more advanced
person. To you and to those who were not antipathetic I spoke
more freely. When the splits in the Order itself became more
and more pronounced my work with 3 others having become
extremely interesting we resolved to carry out a plan suggested
by an Egyptian for the holding together of a strong nucleus
on purely Order lines. This was done by using the symbol of
the globular Sephiroth: formulating it regularly once a week,
each of us formulating the whole symbol, so that the strong
should counterbalance the weak, placing it over the Order,
the planet, then gradually increasing in size and imagining the
symbols disposed as in the star maps on the visible universe.
Here we invoked the light from the true Kether that the spirit
of life and growth might be evoked by that light and that the
great guardian wall of the Sephiroth might shed its influence
upon the planet and the Order. This being done the Light was
carefully concentrated upon the earth and upon the Sphere of
the Order and upon our own spheres. This was done regularly
once a week, and members were warned it was to be used for no
purposes of personal desire, but for all. If we invoked the light
upon the evil that was as yet unfitted for transmutation it was
to be prevented from operating by the Great Guardian of the
formula and not one of us has been allowed to work for our own
selfish aims by means of the formula. It is quite true that in my
experience of the working of the Order I have found several
very capable persons who cannot interest themselves in many
of the Order formulas of clairvoyance and divination yet who
were intensely interested in the end I had in view and which
is expressed above, the late Soror Volo[4] being one of them.
Others were interested in the study of the Egyptian religion
but did not take interest in mediaeval symbolism. The Order
passed into an apparently more and more hopeless state. There
appeared no possible way in which it could emerge from the
dishonesties which desecrated its symbols. Endless divisions,

bickerings, and scandals choked its activity. In the meantime the group I had founded and the groups you and others founded continued their work and at last in 1899 the time came. In the early months of 1900 matters were so arranged by the eternal powers that we were freed from the load of dishonesty under which we had been struggling.

All went well until September 1900 when I found everything I proposed was objected to. After a few weeks I discovered that my group which had been working quietly for 3 years was being violently attacked. First on the ground that we used the Order Rooms. It was then arranged that on Mondays and Wednesdays Members should by giving a weeks' notice have the right to engage the rooms for 2 hours at a time. I was very glad of this as I had frequently been unable to go into the rooms myself when other Members were using them and it was a convenience all round to know when this was likely to be the case. I was then accused of keeping valuable information to myself. You will understand I think that with the anti-Egyptian Feeling about I shall still refuse to discuss Egyptian formulae with anyone not specially in sympathy with the ancient Egyptians. As for the working of my group we each sit at home and go through the stages of the invocation, we each simply invoke light upon the perfectly balanced symbol of the Tree of Life projected on a sphere, we do not work at clairvoyance or divination in any special way and I do not admit that we are concealing knowledge from anyone seeing that the whole of the symbol is explained in the Star maps lecture. I have written to you at great length because you are in the country and I have no opportunity of speaking to you. Would you kindly send this letter to Soror Veritas Vincit.[5] I have recently put up the following notice at 36 B[lythe] R[oad].

S.S.D.D. wishes to say that any Member of the Order who feels sympathy either for the study of the Egyptian Book of the Dead or for the symbolism of the Tree of Life projected on a Sphere will be very welcome to join her group on their attainment of the grade of Theoricus [Adeptus Minor].

Yours under the wings of the eternal O,
Sapientia Sapienti Dono Date, 5°=6° T.A.M.

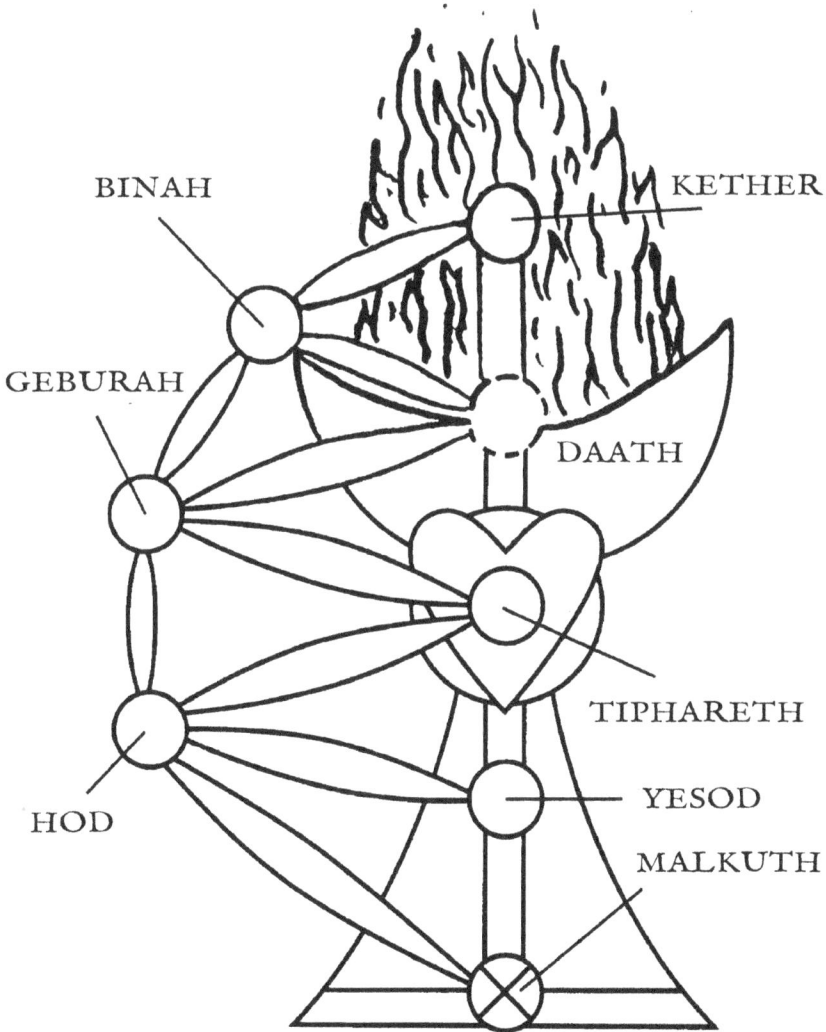

The Cup of the Stolistes

[In March 1901, Florence Farr issued another statement of the "semi-official workings" of the Sphere Group to its Theoricus Adeptus Minor members which was an attempt to clarify the workings of the Group. In this document Farr stated that the Sphere Group no longer had any connection to the Egyptian Adept of the first incarnation of the Sphere Group. According to R.W. Felkin the members of the Sphere Group were informed at a meeting that the Egyptian Adept "was changing his place on the higher planes and could no longer work with us." A second incarnation of the Sphere Group was formed having replaced the Egyptian Adept with an image of the Holy Grail on the central pillar which was called "The Cup of the Stolistes."–D.K.]

The Working of Sphere Group (No. 2)[6]

There were twelve people in the "Sphere Working," evenly divided into six women and six men. Every Sunday from noon to 1 P.M., in their own separate homes but working simultaneously they began by creating an image of the Cup of the Stolistes (Holy Grail) containing a burning heart that represented Tiphareth. The Sephiroth of the "middle pillar" (Kether, Daäth, Tiphareth, Yesod, and Malkuth) were aligned on a central column, with Kether envisioned as a flame arising from the top of the Cup and Malkuth forming its base. The remaining six Sephiroth were doubled (to form twelve) and arched toward the four directions, creating a sphere around Tiphareth. Each person took one of the twelve sphere positions, envisioning themselves not only as the corresponding Sephirah but as an entire Tree of Life within that Sephirah. They saw themselves clothed in the colour of the planet, bathed in an aura the colour of the Sephirah, and they consciously projected appropriately coloured rays of light to the nearest Sephiroth on the central column and to the Sephiroth above and below them. This was a feat of tremendous concentration and visualization ability in itself, but the work was only beginning.

First they imagined that the Sephiroth projected on the sphere were each approximately ten feet in diameter. This image was projected astrally over the Second Order headquarters at 36 Blythe Road. Then they imagined a larger sphere formed over all of London, with each Sephirah one mile in diameter. Next they formed an even larger sphere, 2,700 miles in diameter, over Europe. Fourth, they formed a sphere around the Earth, with Kether over the North Pole and Malkuth over the South Pole. In the fifth operation, the complete solar system (Sun, Moon, and Planets) was placed in the centre Sephirah of Tiphareth and the other Sephiroth, each 900 miles in diameter, were placed in the starry universe and aligned with specific constellations.

Each individual then linked him or herself from their own Kether to the Sphere's Kether via a cord of diamond light through which they travelled to the flaming Crown at the top of the Grail. From Kether they all sent rays of light into the whole universe, the planet, the Order, and themselves. Each individual then returned to his or her own Sephirah and began the journey back to earth, deliberately treading underfoot the shadows known as qliphoth that could potentially generate evil. Thus they transmuted evil into good through the actions of the greater forces on the lesser.

Notes:
1. This letter is reprinted below from George Harper's *Yeats Golden Dawn*, (1974), pp. 221-223.–D.K.
2. Frater Sub Spe was the Second Order motto of J.W. Brodie-Innes.–D.K.
3. Deo Duce Comite Ferro was S.L. Mathers' 7°=4° motto..–D.K.
4. Soror Volo was the Second Order motto of Florence Kennedy.–D.K.
5. Soror Veritas Vincit was the Second Order motto of Mrs. Agnes Cathcart.–D.K.
6. The working of the Sphere Group (No. 2) is based upon the version printed in Mary K. Greer's *Women of the Golden Dawn*, (1995) p. 257.–D.K.

The Way of Wisdom

By Florence Farr Emery

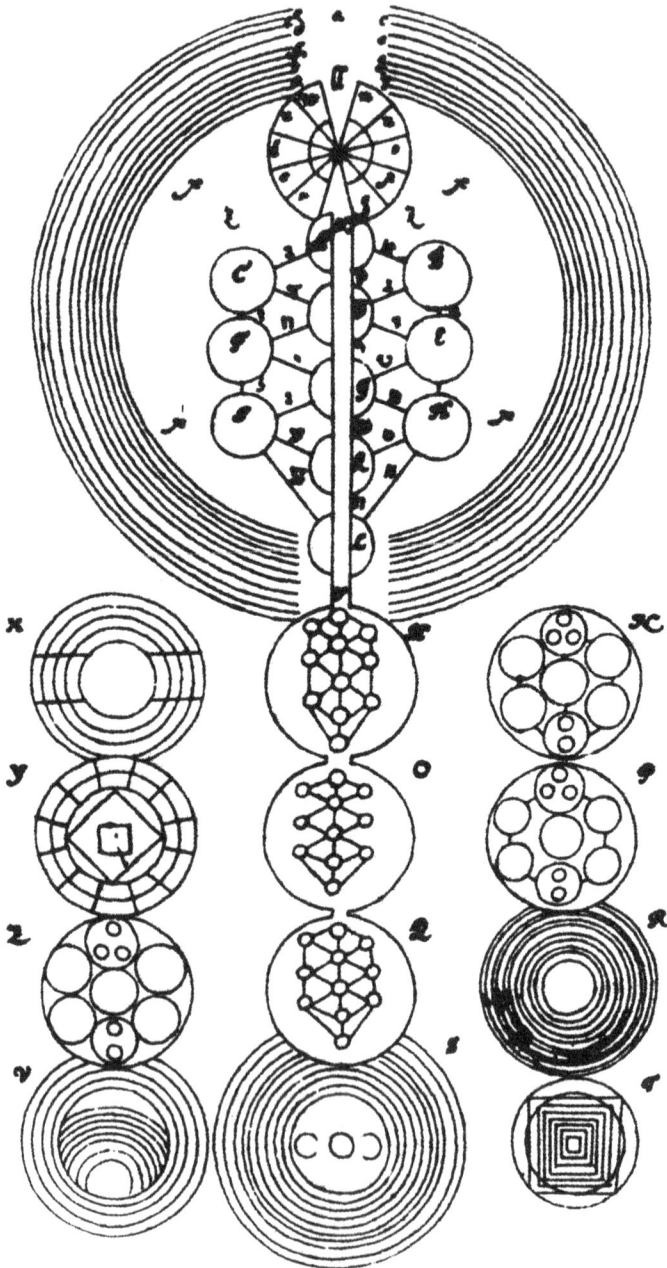

Rosenroth's Gradual Developmental of the Sephiroth
Kabbala Denudata, (1677-84)

The Way of Wisdom:

An Investigation of the Meanings of the Letters of the Hebrew Alphabet Considered as a Remnant of Chaldean Wisdom

By Florence Farr Emery

2012
GOLDEN DAWN RESEARCH TRUST

The Way of Wisdom, originally entitled *The Crucifixion of the Rose*, was first published in this edition by The Golden Dawn Research Trust in 2012.

It was first published by J.M. Watkins in 1900 .

The cover illustration 'The Angel of Osiris' is from Florence Farr's personal copy of *The Book of the Concourse of the Forces*.

The Way of Wisdom[1]

For many centuries the mystery of the Kabbalists has puzzled occult students. Solutions have been offered both in print and by Masters of mystical schools, but none have done more than substitute incomprehensible for incomprehensible.

Some fellow students have found my own solution of use, so I have determined to explain it at length, in the hope it may be of assistance to others. I should say at once that this branch of study is only of interest because the Jews have preserved some of the ancient Chaldean mysteries, and the Great Truths are not to be connected with the tribal worship of Jehovah.

I will first give a list of the words which express the letters of the Hebrew Alphabet and their accepted meanings.

Aleph, an ox; Beth, a house; Gimel, a camel; Daleth, a door; Heh, a window; Vav, a hook; Zayin, armour and sword; Cheth, a fence; Teth, a snake; Yod, a hand; Kaph, a fist; Lamed, an ox-goad; Mem, water; Nun, a fish; Samech, a prop; Ayin, an eye; Peh, a mouth; Tzaddi, a fish hook; Qoph, back of head, car; Resh, a head; Shin, a tooth; Tau, a cross.

These meanings were so unsuggestive that I never even thought of finding the key to the mystery of the God of Letters in this direction, until the idea came that it might be as well to search out the words and see how their root meanings could be applied.

I collected these from my Hebrew lexicon, published in 1828 by James Duncan, 37, Paternoster Row, by an anonymous author. On comparing my results with the last 22 paths of the 32 Paths of Wisdom, published with the *Sepher Yetzirah* by the Theosophical Society in 1893, I found a most interesting relation existed between the two. This I now propose to give in detail.

The opening sentences of the *Sepher Yetzirah* are as follows:

"In 32 wonderful paths of wisdom did God engrave his name. Ten numbers are the ineffable Sephiroth, 22 letters are the foundation of all things."

I therefore allotted the first 10 of the 32 Paths of Wisdom to the 10 numerals [or Sephiroth], and commencing at the 11th Path, compared it with ALEPH the first letter of the Hebrew alphabet as follows:—

"The 11th Path is the Scintillating Intelligence, because it is the essence of the veil which is placed close to the order of the dispositions. This is a special dignity given to it, enabling it to stand before the face of the Cause of Causes."

"A, ALEPH.—The root meaning of which is a leader, chief, pioneer."

The stimulating idea which is akin to the first impulse of creation.

"The 12th Path is the Intelligence of Transparency because it is the kind of high thinking called seership, named 'the place whence issue visions.' "

"B, BETH.—A receptacle, container, bath, box, house."

The seeing of visions has from time immemorial been aided by the enclosure in a Shrine or curtained cupboard of a medium, either in the form of an image, elemental substances, or an actual human being.

"The 13th Path is called the Uniting Intelligence, because it is the essence of glory. It is the fulfilment of the truth of individual spiritual things."

"G, GIMEL.—A harvest, yield, return, requital, a camel, because of its revengeful temper. Ripe fruit falling to the earth from whence it came. Fulfilment of the law that what ye sow in one incarnation ye shall reap in another. The astral body formed by the Lords of retribution."

THE HEBREW ALPHABET

Letter	Power	Value	Final	Name	Meaning
א	A	1		Aleph	Ox
ב	B,V	2		Beth	House
ג	G,Gh	3		Gimel	Camel
ד	D,Dh	4		Daleth	Door
ה	H	5		He	Window
ו	O,U,V	6		Vau	Pin or Hook
ז	Z	7		Zayin	Sword or Armour
ח	Ch	8		Cheth	Fence, Enclosure
ט	T	9		Teth	Snake
י	I,Y	10		Yod	Hand
כ	K,Kh	20, 500	ך	Kaph	Fist
ל	L	30		Lamed	Ox Goad
מ	M	40, 600	ם	Mem	Water
נ	N	50, 700	ן	Nun	Fish
ס	S	60		Samekh	Prop
ע	Aa,Ngh	70		Ayin	Eye
פ	P,Ph	80, 800	ף	Pe	Mouth
צ	Tz	90, 900	ץ	Tzaddi	Fish-hook
ק	Q	100		Qoph	Ear. Back of head
ר	R	200		Resh	Head
ש	S,Sh	300		Shin	Tooth
ת	T,Th	400		Tau	Cross

"The 14th Path is the Illuminating Intelligence, because it is the shining flame which begins the hidden and root ideas of holiness and of their stages of preparation."

"D, DALETH.—To draw from, exhaust, leanness, a door because it is thin, the leaves of a book."

Anyone who has used fasting as a preparation for the reception of ideas, has probably experienced the exultation of sacrifice which is the reward of this exercise. In the flame of the spirit the body is wasted away, and the ideas take form in the mind. The flame of the passions which waste away the body.

"The 15th Path is the Constituting Intelligence, because it forms the substance of creation in pure darkness."

"H, HEH.—To be, to exist."

The first step in evolution from the Absolute.

"The 16th Path is the Triumphal or Eternal Intelligence, because it is the bliss of the glory of glories. It is called the Paradise prepared for the righteous."

"V, Vav.—The link, uniter, hook, chain."

Herein appears to reside the mystery of Devachan, and of the link of identity between incarnation and incarnation.

"The 17th Path is the Disposing Intelligence, because it gives faith to the good, and clothes them with the Holy Spirit or Breath. It is called the beginning of perfection in the state of higher things."

"Z, Zayin.—To be prepared, zone of protection, armour and sword. Also love for the sake of emotion without the hope of fruitfulness."

The arrangement of protective forces perhaps connected with the atmosphere of a planet which is necessary to the perfection of growth. This makes conscious life as we know it possible.

"The 18th Path is the House of Inflowing. From the midst of the investigation or encirclement, the arcana and hidden senses are drawn forth. They dwell in its shade and cling to it from the cause of all causes."

"Ch, Cheth.—To encircle with a cord, to nourish, make fat."

The wearing of a cord has been practised by the Brahmins, Parsees, and monks of all denominations. The drawing forth and nourishment of the arcana or secret names and forms is beyond doubt the object of the very general custom.

"The 19th Path, the Intelligence of all the Activities of Spiritual Beings; because of the out-flowing diffused by it from the most high blessing and the most exalted sublime glory."

"T, Teth.—A snake, a basket."

In the Mysteries of Demeter the priestesses carried baskets through the streets, which were supposed to contain sacred serpents. In Egypt the Uraeus serpent was always depicted coiled for a spring over the festival basket. This most occult of symbols we find by this key to denote the flow of force from the operator through the channels of sense.

"The 20ᵗʰ Path is the Intelligence of Will, because it is the means of preparation of each created being: by it the existence of primordial wisdom becomes known."

"I, Y, Yod.—The active agent, to cast forth, power."

Will is diffused throughout the universe; conscious or unconscious, it is with us in all our parts, and in all the migrations of our mind. If we can grasp the nature of abstract Will we shall understand the being which was wise before the boundary of matter enclosed it.

"The 21ˢᵗ Path is the Intelligence of Conciliation, because it receives the divine influence, which flows into it from its benediction upon all existence."

"K, Kaph.—Appeasing wrath, cup, cave, pelvis."

The redeeming symbol of the Grail seems clearly indicated by this. That attitude of Aspiration through which the Higher Mind can be evoked.

"The 22ⁿᵈ Path is the Faithful Intelligence, because by it spiritual virtues are increased, and nearly all dwellers on earth are under its shadow."

"L, Lamed.—Accustomed, scholar, a trained disciple; the goad."

The goad is a well-established means of discipline, and self-castigation has been frequently practised by ascetics. This is a way of wisdom which is apt to make a man a follower rather than a leader, and is certainly of the nature of a lesser good. Symbolised on the Ajanta Fresco found in the Buddhist caves as an arrow piercing the eye.

"The 23rd Path is the Stable Intelligence, because it has the virtue of consistency among all numerations."

"M, Mem.—The atom, a spot, the least thing, the subject of the discourse."

The elemental atom has a continuous existence in spite of many changes of form. It is invisible to us.

"The 24th Path is the Imaginative Intelligence, because it gives a likeness to all similar objects created after the same fashion."

"N, Nun.—Propagation." (By budding or division as in protoplasm.)

The transmission of tendencies through the image-forming thought.

"The 25th Path is the Probationary Intelligence, because it is the primary temptation by which the creator trieth all righteous persons."

"S, Samech.—A tree, a support."

Evidently connected with the equilibrium so often inculcated in ethical systems. In the Ajanta Fresco, a human being is gathering fruit from a tree and storing it in a basket.

"The 26th Path is the Renovating Intelligence, because the Holy God renews by it all the changing things which are renewed by the creation of the world."

"Aa, Ayin.—The reflected image in an eye, a cloud, a reply; also love with the intention of producing offspring in contrast to the love symbolised by Zayin."

It is interesting to note that frequently the first phenomenon noticed by a crystal gazer is that a cloud forms and a vision is seen in the midst of the cloud.

"The 27th Path is the Exciting Intelligence. By it is created the intellect of all created beings under the highest heaven and the excitement or motion of them."

"P, Peh.—Assent, agreement, turning towards, harmony."

Sympathy or "feeling with" what is outside one's circle of interests, stimulates the intellect because it increases the power of understanding, that which is beyond the personality. The harmony can only be received by the higher or more universal mind.

"The 28th Path is the Natural Intelligence, because through it is consummated and perfected the nature of every existing being under the orb of the sun."

"Tz, Tzaddi.—To lie in wait, to hunt, to hide in and spring out from a narrow defile; as in birth the child springs forth."

The spirit of enterprise which gives the power of springing forth new-born, as it were, in the hunt for experience.

"The 29th Path is the Corporeal Intelligence, because it forms every body which is formed beneath the whole set of worlds and the increment of them."

"Q, Qoph.—Darkness, coagulation, solidification."

The making visible of matter through concentration. Everyone knows that the radiant star dust of matter is first what is called etheric, then gaseous, and as it gradually cools and coagulates, it becomes liquid and finally solid.

"The 30th Path is the Collecting Intelligence, because astrologers deduce from it the judgment of the stars and the celestial signs."

"R, Resh.—Destitution, poverty, emptiness."

Pulsation may be set in motion by the creation of a vacuum. This formula is one probably employed by the sages who tabulated the effects of the fixed stars. In the power of creating a vacuum dwells the mystery of the voice of the silence, and of the unknown powers that await us in the beyond.

"The 31st Path is the perpetual intelligence, because it regulates the motions of the sun and moon in their proper order, each in an orbit convenient for it."

"Sh, SHIN.–That which repeats, or goes over the same ground again, a male, a tooth because it is renewed."

The cycles of the year and the month. This tendency to repeat is the third of the great mother qualities inherent in the plane of formulation.

"The 32nd Path is the administrative intelligence, because it directs and associates in all their operations, the seven planets."

"T, TAU.–A limit, a boundary, a room, a cross."

The orbit of the outermost planet. The end. The Stone of the Wise. The crystallisation of the perfected work; excessively evil if it takes place prematurely. A useful analogy is the aptness of carbon to crystallise as graphite, and its inaptness to crystallise as diamond.

I must now consider the 22 letters in the Kabbalistic groups.

A, M, SH, are the 3 Mother letters.

B, G, D, K, P, R, TAU, are the 7 Double letters.

H, V, Z, CH, TETH, I, L, N, S, AA, TZ, Q, are the 12 Simple letters.

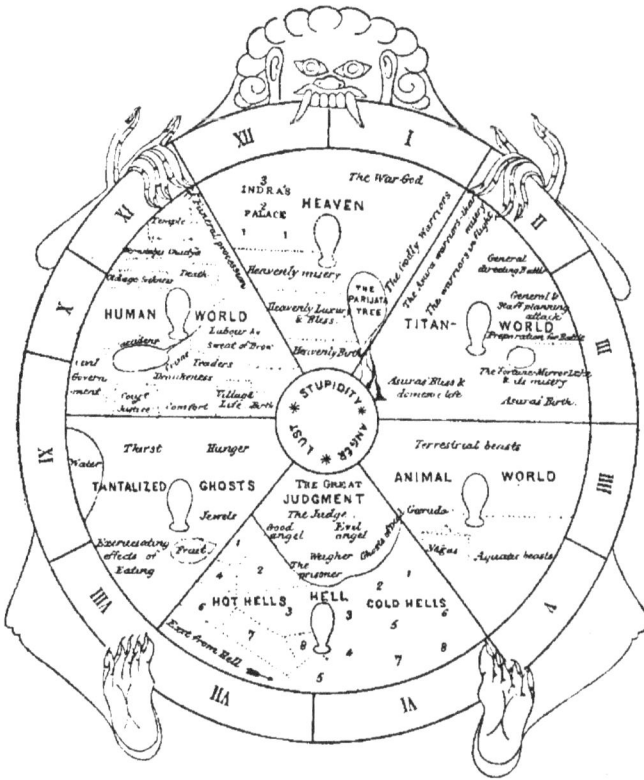

The Buddhist Wheel of Existence

M (Mem), as I say above, is the Stable Intelligence, and its radical meaning is "the least thing possible" or "the subject of the discourse." Now the Hebrew Alphabet is a discourse on the method of manifestation or formation. The smallest manifest thing is an atom. I will therefore assume that M means atomic or invisible matter. Aleph is the chief or leader; this implies action. The action of atoms is at first anabolic or building up, living at a profit, a feminine tendency: and afterwards katabolic or living at a waste, a masculine tendency. (This is gone into at great length by Geddes and Thomson in *The Evolution of Sex*.) The oscillation is initiated by the Aleph force but it is repeated over and over again by the great force of Shin which might well be called the mother of cycles or repetitions.

The 7 double letters are all of a passive receptive nature. They correspond to the seven tattvas and human forms thus: BETH, physical body, earth; GIMEL, astral image, water; DALETH, passional body, fire; KAPH, receptive mind-form, air; PEH, inspiring mind-form, ether; RESH, ideal form, divine flame; TAU, the completed atomic vehicle; Akasha.

Let us now compare these attributions which are given in technical language in the III (third) volume of Blavatsky's *The Secret Doctrine,* to the root meaning of the Hebrew.

B, the body as a shrine for the spirit. G, the result of the past. D, the lean body of desire. K, a cup, the lower mind. P, the harmonious circling of the higher mind. R, a vacuum, the place of the voice of the silence. TAU, a boundary, the egg-shaped vehicle of light or darkness.

If we are to allot these seven double letters to Planets and all the other correspondences of the number, we can avoid the error of regarding them as anything but vehicles for the 12 activities that are symbolised by the Zodiac, and for the 10 numerals hidden behind the veil.

In speaking of the twelve Simple letters it will be useful to compare their meanings as given above with the 12 symbols on the Buddhist Wheel of Existence, discovered by Surgeon Major Waddell, in a fresco at Ajanta. See L.A. Waddell's *The Buddhism of Tibet,* page 108. This wheel is of Chaldean origin, although it has been overlaid with Buddhist symbolism.

There are 12 drawings round the wheel, illustrating the following stages in existence:—

AVIDYA.—Being broods on the thought that nothing exists. This is the state corresponding to HEH, Being.

SANSKARA.—Action of Karma, the fruit of the past and seed of the future, otherwise VAV, the link.

VIJNANA.—The dawn of self-consciousness. ZAYIN.—The protecting covering of the Great Breath, the atmosphere or mirror of life.

Waddell's Buddhist Wheel of Existence

NAMA-RUPA.—The separation of subject and object. Name and form. CHETH.—Forms in-flowing from the binding of the cord.

CHADAYATANA.—Rushing outwards through the channels of sense. TETH.—The serpentine convolutions from the interior to the exterior.

SPARSA.—Contract. YOD.—The activity of the Will.

Vebana.—Consciousness of sensation. Lamed.—Gained by repetition or practice.

Trishna.—Pleasure or pain. Nun.—Propagation.

Upadana.—Fruit, accumulating. Samech.—The sustaining temptation. The picture is of a man grasping fruit by a tree.

Bhava.—Fertile woman. Ayin.—Renovation of changing life.

Jati.—Birth. Tzaddi.—Hiding, lying in wait in a narrow place.

Jakamakana.—Death. Qoph.—Darkness.

In the pictorial diagram of human life, as conceived by Buddhist philosophy, the causal nexus begins at the left-hand side of the top partition. The twelve links round the rim follow in the usual order and in evolutionary fashion as follows :—

CAUSAL CATEGORY.	SANSKRIT.	EVOLUTIONARY STAGE.
I. Unconscious Will	Avidyā	Stage of passing from Death to Re-birth.
II. Conformations	Sanskara	Shaping of formless physical and mental materials (in the Gāta).
III. Consciousness	Vijñāna	Rise of Conscious Experience.
IV. Self-consciousness	Nama-rupa	Rise of Individuality—distinction between self and not-self.
V. Sense-surfaces and Understanding	Chadāyatana	Realizes possession of Sense-Surfaces and Understanding with reference to outside world.
VI. Contact	Sparşa	Exercise of Sense-organs on outer world.
VII. Feeling	Vedanā	Mental and physical sensations.
VIII. Desire	Trishņā	Desire, as experience of pain or delusive pleasure.
IX. Indulgence	Upādāna	Grasping greed, as satisfying Desire, inducing clinging to Worldly Wealth and desire of heir to it.
X. Fuller Life	Bhava	Life in fuller form, as enriched by satisfying desire of married life and as means of obtaining heir.
XI. Birth (of heir)	Jāti	Maturity by birth of heir (which affords re-birth to another spirit).
XII. Decay and Death.	Jarāmaraņa	Maturity leads to Decay and to Death.
I. Unconscious Will.	Avidyā	Passing from Death to Re-birth.

191

The *Theosophical Review* printed a detailed account of the Buddhist Wheel of Life, in the summer numbers of the year 1899, and I regret I cannot do more here than roughly indicate the interesting analogy to be discovered in the Semitic and Buddhist records of the ancient Chaldean system of evolution.

The 7 vehicles expressed by the 7 letters, can with a little study, be allotted to the 7 abodes pictured between the spokes of the Wheel of Life, and said to be inhabited by Gods, Titans, Men, Animals, The Judge, The Demons, and The Tantalised Ghosts. Explained by Madame Blavatsky to mean the High Gods, the Father Gods, the Guardian Gods, the Boddhisattvas, men in the underworld, men or animals in the astral.

Round the axle of the Wheel revolve a cock, a serpent, and a black pig. The red cock symbolises a leader, initiative impulse; the green serpent the repetition of the cycles, and the black pig matter in its invisible or atomic form. These answer to the 3 mother letters.

In conclusion, I will give an example of a method of interpretation which Mr. Skinner has already explained to the uninitiated world in his *Source of Measures*. It is to take a Hebrew word and make a sentence from the elemental meaning of the letters composing it.

The first words of the Book of Genesis are Berashith Bera Elohim, spell in Hebrew בְּרֵאשִׁית בָּרָא אֱלֹהִים (B R A Sh I Th B R A   A L H I M), translaed, "In the beginning the Gods created."

From what has been said above it is clear that we may attribute the following meanings to the various letters:—

Beth.—A shrine, a dwelling; Resh.—A vacuum; Aleph.—Stimulating idea; Shin.— Repeaters, followers; Yod.—Active agent, Will; Tau.—Boundary, enclosure, envelope.

Dwelling in the vacuum was the stimulating idea (Aleph), the repeaters forming a boundary, or we may, write it thus: Dwelling in the vacuum was the stimulating idea, the will repeating the first impulse formed a boundary.

Here we have a description of the first pulsation in the nebulous star dust we call a universe; or again, the nucleus and limiting membrane of a protoplasmic cell.

Bra emphasises the first part of this description, and shows the pulsation vibrated twice from the stimulating idea.

Alohim is the word usually translated for God, but being plural it should be Gods.

Aleph, stimulation. Lamed, training, teaching, goading on.

Heh, existence becoming. Yod, active agent. Mem, the atoms of invisible matter.

These are the spiritual forces to be understood by the Elohim, who "created in the beginning."
Their permutations in the process are expressed by other divine names, such as Al, Ih, Ahih, and so forth.
The study of the Alphabet leaves us still in the dark as to the exact nature of the stimulating impulse symbolised by Aleph, but a further study of the numerals or forces "behind the veil" solves the riddle to a great extent, and I will explain them later.
We must never forget in working out these interpretations that the mysteries of the 22 letters are those of the World of Formation, the world in which the invisible pattern of the universe was made; and that behind the letters are the mysteries of the numbers, and behind the numbers the circle, the Great Breath, Eternal and Abiding in Perfection.

NOTE:

Some or my readers have, I believe, made a special study of Daniel v. 25, and his interpretation of the writing on the wall. Read by aid of this key a somewhat interesting result is obtained from the roots of the words "Mene Mene Teqel Upharsin." M, N, A. M, the subject of the discourse, Belshazzar. N, as a verb, gives: has impressed similitudes of himself. A, as the object, gives: upon the primal impulses of formation. Tau, Q, L.— Tau, his limitation, Q, has darkened, L, those subject to his discipline. P, R, S.—P, it is agreed. R, to make empty, to remove. S, his supports.

Belshazzar has imposed his personality upon the highest fountain of impulse. His limitation has kept his subjects in the darkness of ignorance. It is agreed that that which supported him shall be removed.

A Calendar of Philosophy

Edited by
Florence Farr
from the Works of
Great
Writers.

London: Frank Palmer

A Calendar of Philosophy

A
CALENDAR
OF
PHILOSOPHY

EDITED BY

FLORENCE FARR

FROM THE WORKS OF

GREAT WRITERS

PAGE DESIGNS
& COVER BY
W. S. LEAR

2012
GOLDEN DAWN RESEARCH TRUST

A Calendar of Philosophy was first published in 1910 by Frank Palmer, London.

This edition was published by The Golden Dawn Research Trust in 2012.

JANUARY

WILL'E.LEAR.MO

January the First
All is Laughter,
all is Dust.
GLYCON

Calendar of Philosophy

January 2.

Few I know will snarl at the liberty of my writings that have not more cause to snarl at their thought's looseness.— *Montaigne.*

January 3.

The Devil was the first reformer.— *Sidney Smith.*

January 4.

You never know what is enough unless you know what is more than enough.— *William Blake.*

January 5.

What art thou, Man, and why art thou despairing? God shall forgive thee all but thy despair.— *Myers.*

January 6.

Doubt of all kinds can be removed by nothing but action.— *Goethe.*

January 7.

He abhorred those innocent souls to whom the very difficult appears impossible.— *Gracian, Spanish.*

January 8.

Mankind weep for the dead when they should mourn for the flower of youth perishing.— *Theognis.*

January 9.

When we look outward we see in each other forms and colours and bodies; when we turn within we feel the breath of the spirit circling in our minds. The eye which can see that forms and spirits are the same is the very Axis of Tao (the Gnosis). And when that Axis passes through the centre in which all Infinites converge simples and complexes are known to be as one.— *Hui Tzu.*

January 10.

Country life is very good; in fact, the best-for cattle.—
Sidney Smith.

January 11.

At first true love is akin to the clouds which hold lightning
in their folds, later in its day it becomes of like nature to the
serene blue sky.—*Anonymous.*

January 12.

What is life a tale that is told;
    What is life? a frenzy extreme;
    A shadow of things that seem,
And the greatest good is but small
That all life is a dream to all,
    And that dreams themselves are a dream.
                                    —*Calderon.*

January 13.

Our life consisteth partly of folly and partly in wisdom.
He that writes of it but reverently and regularly omits the
better moiety of it.—*Montaigne.*

January 14.

Dionysus was the son of Semele, a woman, but Eros is the
son of the goddess. His ecstasy is not a sudden intoxication,
it is not shattered when the dance and wine are finished; it
is a gift which remains with us for ever.—*Anonymous.*

January 15.

The tigers of wrath are wiser than the horses of
instruction.—*William Blake.*

January 16.

Nature holds illusions before one, because she knows the
gifts she has to give are not worth troubling about. —*W. B.*
Yeats.

January 17.

You say that a good cause will even justify war. I tell you that a good war will justify any cause. — *Nietzsche.*

January 18.

Work makes the comrade. — *Goethe.*

January 19.

Whomsoever I behold with attention doth easily convey and imprint something of his in me. What I heedily consider, the same I usurp. — *Montaigne.*

January 20.

Nature is miracle all. She knows no laws; the same returns not, save to bring the different. The slow round of the engraver's lathe gains but the breadth of a hair, but the difference is distributed back over the whole curve, never an instant true — ever not quite. There are no fortunes to be told and there is no advice to be given. Farewell. — *Benjamin Blood.*

January 21.

A woman's advice is of small account, and he who does not take it is of no account. — *Cervantes.*

January 22.

We are alive here to build bridges and roads that the everlasting may know mortal life and that mortals may remember their own infinitude. I believe in that work. — *Anonymous.*

January 23.

To combat an opinion is as often as not to strengthen it; if you would really destroy it, do homage to it and then interpret skilfully. — *A. E. Waite.*

January 24.

Some strand of our own misdoing is involved in every quarrel. — *R. L. Stevenson.*

January 25.

The man who cannot forgive any mortal thing is a green hand in life.—*R. L. Stevenson.*

January 26.

He who has suffered you to impose on him, knows you.—*William Blake.*

January 27.

Some god within you has converted you to ungodliness.—*Nietzsche.*

January 28.

Moral sentiment, like cleanliness, should be practised in private.—*A. E. Waite.*

January 29.

I love a good dressing before any beauty in the world. A woman is then like a delicate garden; nor is there any one kind of it; she may vary every hour.—*Ben Jonson.*

January 30.

There is not a quaint phrase, nor a choice word, nor ambiguous figure, nor pathetical example, nor alluring posture, but women know them all better than our books: it is a cunning bred in their veins and will never out of the flesh.—*Montaigne.*

January 31.

We should guard against a talent which we cannot hope to practise in perfection.—*Goethe.*

February 1.

What is wrong with the world is that the artist who created it was too pleased with his first attempts.—*Anonymous.*

February 2.

The final fact of human nature is emotion, crystallising itself in thought and language, eternalising itself in action and art.—*John Addington Symonds.*

February 3.

One alone, who is a master of vice, can corrupt a whole people.—*Fernan de Rojas.*

February 4.

If I buy a woman I get her arts and deceptions; if I interest a woman I get her admiration; if I give her myself she becomes the symbol of immortal beauty and nothing she can do can deprive me of my dream.—*Anonymous.*

February 5.

Behind the proudest consciousness that ever reigned wisdom and wonder blushed face to face. Inevitable, solitary, and safe in one sense, but queer and cactus-like in another sense.—*Benjamin Blood.*

February 6.

What are thoughts but pale dead feelings?—*Novalis.*

February 7.

Nature apart from Science is like a great romance, full of mystery and high seeming, produced in a Gothic folio, with a cover of hide and antique clasps of metal; but Nature as scrutinised by Science is like the text of the same romance edited by a member of a folk-lore society.—*A. E. Waite.*

February 8.

The liberality of ladies is too profuse in marriage and blunts the edge of affection and desire.—*Montaigne.*

February 9.

The fox provides for himself, but God provides for the lion.—*William Blake.*

February 10.

I always knew that the line of Nature is crooked, that though we dig the canal beds as straight as we can, the rivers run hither and thither in their wildness.—*W. B. Yeats.*

February 11.

Let no one suppose that the world has been waiting for him to save it.—*Goethe.*

February 12.

From a psalm of Asaph to a seat at the London opera in the Haymarket what a road have men travelled.—*Carlyle.*

February 13.

In peace and prosperity States and individuals have better sentiments, because they are not confronted with imperious necessities; but war takes away the easy supply of men's wants, and so proves a hard task-master, which brings most men's character to a level with their fortunes.—*Thucydides.*

February 14.

The friend that flattereth, weakeneth at length;
It is the foe that calleth forth our strength.
　　　　　　　　　—*George Meredith*

February 15.

A man is never deserted until he forsakes himself.—*A. E. Waite.*

February 16.

I believe that the borders of our minds are ever shifting, and that many minds can flow into one another, as it were, and create or reveal a single mind.—*W. B. Yeats.*

February 17.

Valour is the enemy's first battalion.—*Calderon.*

February 18.

I willingly imitate that painter who, having bungler-like drawn and fondly represented some cocks, forbade his boys to suffer any live cock to come into his shop.—*Montaigne.*

February 19.

All that is human has become unlawful since the seer of Galilee became ruler of the world. With him to live means to die. Love and hatred both are sins. Has he then transformed men's flesh and blood? Has not earth-bound man remained what he ever was? Our healthy souls rebel against it all; and yet we are to will in the very teeth of our own will.—*Julian the Apostate.*

February 20.

There is not the least use in preaching to anyone unless you chance to catch them ill.—*Sidney Smith.*

February 21.

One feels sometimes that Rossetti desired a world of essences, of unmixed powers, of impossible purities. It is as though the last judgment had already begun in his mind; and the essence and powers which the divine hand had mixed with one another to make the loam of life, fell asunder at his touch.—*W. B. Yeats.*

February 22.

Great literature is indeed the forgiveness of sin, and when we find it becoming the accusation of sin, as in George Eliot, who plucks her *Tito* in pieces with as much assurance as if he had been clockwork, literature has begun to change into something else.—*W. B. Yeats.*

February 23.

Most people feel with their fingers rather than with their nerves, with their nerves rather than with their brains, with their brains rather than with their imaginations.—*Anonymous.*

February 24.

For who would live in chronicles renowned
Must combat folly, or as fool be crowned.
                              —*George Meredith.*

February 25.

The destiny of the greater part of the human race is either infinitely pathetic or infinitely ridiculous. Under which aspect shall such destinies be considered? Villiers de L'Isle Adam was too sincere an idealist to hesitate. "As for living," he cries in that splendid phrase of Axël, "our servants will do that for us!"—*Arthur Symons.*

February 26.

Wedlock hath for his share honour, justice, profit, and constancy, a plain but general delight. Love melts in only pleasure; and truly it hath it, more lively, more quaint, and more sharp, a pleasure inflamed by difficulty. There must be a kind of stinging tingling and smarting. It is no longer love if it once be without arrows and without fire.—*Montaigne.*

February 27.

I kissed her again with a thundering kiss. Oh, what a peacemaker that is! It is the mediator, the guarantee, the umpire, the Bond of Union, the Solemn League and Covenant, the Plenipotentiary, the Aaron's Rod, the Jacob's Staff, the Prophet Elisha's Pot of Oil, the Philosopher's Stone, the Horn of Plenty, and the Tree of Life between man and woman.— *Letter from Robert Burns altered by W. Bell Scott.*

February 28.

I am not fond of expecting catastrophes, but there are cracks in the world.—*Sidney Smith.*

March 1.

Why do people say it is prosaic to get inspiration out of wine? Is it not the sunlight and the sap in the leaves? Are not grapes made by the sunlight and the sap?— *William Morris.*

March 2.

History is the biography of great men.—*Carlyle.*

March 3.

Build a bridge of silver for the flying foe.—*Cervantes.*

March 4.

However philosophic and austere a man is on his own account, he becomes a thief and a plunderer on behalf of his children.—*Anonymous.*

March 5.

Some men can only get respect as a highwayman gets money—by demanding it.—*William Shenstone.*

March 6.

It is the love of dreams which mingles so much bitterness with the dreams of love.—*A. E. Waite.*

March 7.

Certainty is the root of despair. Not unfortunately the universe is wild, game-flavoured as a hawk's wing.—*Benjamin Blood.*

March 8.

Distrust and fear are often born from love and honour.—*Lope de Vega.*

March 9.

Hope and memory must die before we can realise the Everlasting Now.—*Anonymous.*

March 10.

When the soul is exhausted of fire then doth the spirit return unto its primal nature and there is upon it a peace great and of the woodland, then it becometh kin to the faun and the dryad, a woodland dweller amid the rocks and streams.—*James of Basel.*

March 11.

Luxury is like a wild beast first made fiercer with tying and then let loose.—*Montaigne.*

March 12.

The genius of being is whimsical rather than consistent.—
Benjamin Blood.

March 13.

A clear proof of worth is to be able to honour your
enemy.—*Calderon.*

March 14.

There is nothing so ridiculously pitiable as a popular
favourite.—*Anonymous.*

March 15.

When I was a boy I read philosophy and I followed the
teaching of the greatest of philosophers. I became all things
to all men, a thief among thieves, a sage among sages—but
now I am no longer perfectly adaptable. I criticise instead
of comprehending. I am caught in a world of solid things.—
Anonymous.

March 16.

The eagle never lost so much time as when he submitted
to learn of the crow.—*William Blake.*

March 17.

There are things which the intellect can seek, but by
herself will never find. These things instinct can find
but will never seek them unprompted by the intellect.—
Henri Bergson.

March 18.

"Look o'er thine own past follies." "So I do,"
Retorts the wag; "and overlook them too."
                                        —*Horace.*

March 19.

The supremest voluptuousness both ravisheth and
plaineth as doth sorrow.—*Montaigne.*

March 20.

The show is on; and what a show it is if we will but give it our attention! Barbecues, bonfires, and banners? Tyre, Rome, Spain, and Venice also had their day. But there have been high jinks before. Nineveh and We are passing, the news must become less interesting or tremendously more so—a breath can make it, as a breath made it in the beginning.—*Benjamin Blood.*

March 21.

Love turns men into women, women into men.—*Mira de Mescua.*

March 22.

Shapes of beauty which haunt our moments of inspiration, held by most men for the frailest of ephemera, but by Blake for a people older than the world: citizens of Eternity appearing and re-appearing in the minds of artists and poets.—*W. B. Yeats.*

March 23.

Since the French Revolution—since the reign of reason began that is—Englishmen are all intermeasurable one with another. Certainly a happy state of agreement in which I do not agree.—*William Blake.*

March 24.

Alas! it is so much easier to love men while they exist only on paper.—*Carlyle.*

March 25.

If a rainbow lasts a quarter of an hour, no one looks at it any more.—*Goethe.*

March 26.

To Verlaine every corner of the world was alive with tempting and consoling and terrifying beauty. I have never known anyone to whom the sight of the eyes was so intense and imaginative a thing.—*Arthur Symons.*

March 27.

Taste is at first a cultivated instinct, and later on, when the critical and self-conscious spirit develops in a youth, he will recognise and salute it as a friend with whom his education has made him long familiar.—*Plato.*

March 28.

Other men arrange their lives, take sides, follow one direction; Verlaine hesitates before a choice which seems to him monstrous; he cannot resign himself to the necessity of sacrificing doctrine to passion, or passion to doctrine, without a moment's repose he oscillates from one to the other.—*Charles Morice.*

March 29.

"Take eloquence and wring its neck!" Give instead "Sincerity and the impression of the moment followed to the letter."—*Paul Verlaine.*

March 30.

The secret of all comes to us in sudden inspirations and not in evolved systems.—*A. E. Waite.*

March 31.

We have peradventure to blame ourselves for making so foolish a production as man, and to entitle both the deed and parts thereto belonging shameful. What monstrous beast is this that makes himself a horror to himself, whom his delights displease, who ties himself unto misfortune.—*Montaigne.*

APRIL

April the First

The Wise man
gets more from his
Enemies than a Fool
gets from his Friends

GRACIAN

April 2.

Progress? And to what? Time turns a weary and a wistful face. Has he not traversed one eternity? and shall another give the secret up? We have dreamed of a climax and a consummation, a final triumph where a world shall burn *en barbecue;* but there is no purpose in Eternity. It pays mainly as it goes or not at all.—*Benjamin Blood.*

April 3.

The great man who lives too long becomes a bad man. If he does not attain martyrdom the sins of his followers enter into him.—*Anonymous.*

April 4.

No bird soars too high if he soars with his own wings.— *William Blake.*

April 5.

Blake deified imaginative freedom and held corporeal reason for the most accursed of things, because it makes the imagination revolt from the sovereignty of beauty and pass under the sovereignty of corporeal law.—*W. B. Yeats.*

April 6.

In Heaven the angels awake each morning innocent of knowledge; by noon they have learned all wisdom, which towards evening fades gradually from their vision.—*MSS., Sixteenth Century.*

April 7.

"If those who ride applaud, who cares for those who go afoot?" asked Arbuscula, when the mob hissed her acting.— *Horace.*

April 8.

To the heart nothing can speak save another heart.—*Diego de Estella.*

April 9.

In the city cheats, at home cares, in the country toil, at sea fear. Art married?— anxieties. Art unmarried?— lonesomeness. With children?—disturbances. Without?—a crippled life. In youth folly, in old age weakness. Let us never be born, or let us die at birth.—*Posidippus.*

April 10.

In the city gain, at home rest, in the country fresh air, at sea adventure. Art married?—good. Unmarried?—better. With children? — darlings! Art childless? — care is gone. Youth is strong; old age venerable. Let us make haste to live.—*Metrodorus.*

April 11.

The worst educated man is usually your man of fortune. He has not put forth his hand upon anything except the bell-rope.—*Carlyle.*

April 12.

Fear nothing but fear.—*Carlyle.*

April 13.

Re-integration and not individuality is the end of all separate existence.—*A. E. Waite.*

April 14.

When opposing warriors join in battle, he who has pity conquers.—*Lao Tzu.*

April 15.

When Antigenydes the musician was to play any music he gave order that before or after him some other bad musicians should cloy and surfeit his auditory. So gave he himself some lustre or grace.—*Montaigne.*

April 16.

The best wine is the oldest, the best water the newest.— *William Blake.*

April 17.

When a man is capable of lifting his consciousness out of his humanity and can realise his elemental nature, he has gained the Kingdom of Heaven.—*Anonymous.*

April 18.

Those who know do not speak; those who speak do not know. He who acts, destroys; he who grasps, loses.—*Lao Tzu.*

April 19.

That immortal waste-paper basket in which Time carries, with many sighs, the failures of great men.—*W. B. Yeats.*

April 20.

To create a little flower is the labour of ages.—*William Blake.*

April 21.

There is no greater consolation for mediocrity than that genius is not immortal.—*Goethe.*

April 22.

The gods have tired of every shape and size
That goldsmiths could produce or priests devise.
—*Dryden.*

April 23.

There are men who see that Dignity may be disgraced, and who feel that Disgrace may be dignified.—*Bolingbroke.*

April 24.

There can be no purpose in Eternity. It is process all. The most sublime result, if it appeared as ultimatum, would go stale in an hour—it could not be endured.—*Benjamin Blood.*

April 25.

The bowels carry the feet, not feet the bowels.—*Cervantes.*

April 26.

All who look fools are fools—and half the others too.—
Gracian.

April 27.

There are three relationships in human life—commercial,
which depend on what you have; social, which depend upon
what you do; and real, which depend upon what you are. If
you give your possessions you are merchants; if you give
deeds you are heroes; if you give yourselves you are saints
and sages.—*Anonymous.*

April 28.

A fool and his words are soon parted.—*Shenstone.*

April 29.

Nothing is more rare in any man than an act of his own.
—*Emerson.*

April 30.

There is commonly brawling and contention between
men and women, and the nearest consent we have with them
is but stormy and tumultuous.—*Montaigne.*

May 1.

Bashfulness is an ornament to youth, but a reproach to
age.—*Aristotle.*

May 2.

Man unto man is either a god or a wolf.—*Erasmus.*

May 3.

You must treat the public as you treat women: you must
tell them nothing but what you know they would like to
hear.—Goethe.

May 4.

Good authors deject me too, too much and quail my
courage.—*Montaigne.*

May 5.

For she is a good wife, and that a good marriage not that is so indeed, but whereof no man speaketh.— *Montaigne.*

May 6.

It is the wisdom of Heaven not to strive, yet it overcomes; not to speak, yet it obtains a response; it calls not and things come of themselves.—*Lao Tzu.*

May 7.

The apple-tree never asks the beech how he shall grow; nor the lion, the horse how he shall take his prey.—*William Blake.*

May 8.

The Goncourts caught at Impressionism to render the fugitive aspects of a world which existed only as a thing of flat spaces, and angles, and coloured movement, in which sun and shadow were the artists: as moods, no less flitting were the artists of the merely receptive consciousnesses of men and women.—*Arthur Symons.*

May 9.

Flaubert was resolute to be the novelist of a world in which art, formal art, was the only escape from the burden of reality, and in which the soul was of use mainly as the agent of fine literature.—*Arthur Symons.*

May 10.

Man, what thou art is hidden from thyself.
Knowest thou that morning, mid-day and the eve
Are all within thee? The ninth heaven art thou
That from the spheres into the roar of time
Did'st fall erewhile. Thou art the brush that painted
The hues of all the world—the light of life
That ranged its glory in the nothingness.

—*Faridu.*

May 11.

Know, once for all, that there is for thee no other universe than that conception thereof, which is reflected at the bottom of thy thoughts. What is knowledge but a recognition?—*Villiers de L'Isle-Adam.*

May 12.

And in my conceit, he understood it right that said, a good marriage might be made between a blind woman and a deaf man.—*Montaigne.*

May 13.

Production without possession, action without self-assertion, development without domination, this is the mysterious operation of Tao (*wisdom*).—*Lao Tzu.*

May 14.

"It is a man's own breast that makes him eloquent." Our people term judgment language; or full conception fine words. It is the quaintness or liveliness of the conceit that elevates and puffs up the words.—*Montaigne.*

May 15.

Living in a time when technique and imagination are continually perfect and complete because they no longer strive to bring fire from Heaven, we forget how imperfect and incomplete they were even in the greatest masters, in Botticelli, in Arcagna, and in Giotto.—*W. B. Yeats.*

May 16.

Listen to the fool's reproach. It is a kingly title.—*William Blake.*

May 17.

Intense impudence is the true philosopher's stone.—*Douglas Jerrold.*

May 18.

Spirit and matter have been presented to us in the rudest contrast, the one as all noble, the other as all vile. Suppose we learn to consider them as opposite faces of the self-same mystery. . . . Looking at matter not as brute matter, but as the living garment of God.—*Tyndall's Belfast Address.*

May 19.

Love is an affair of two, and is only for two that can be as quick, as constant in intercommunication, as are sun and earth, through the cloud or face to face. They take their breath of life from one another in signs of affection, proofs of faithfulness, incentiveness to admiration. Thus it is with men and women in love's good season. But a solitary soul dragging a log must make the log a god to rejoice in the burden. That is not love.—*George Meredith.*

May 20.

Perhaps it speaks well for human nature on the whole that people are so surprised to find themselves odious to others.—*George Eliot.*

May 21.

The living, rather than the dead, walk in a world of phantoms.—*Gerard de Nerval.*

May 22.

The imagined is greater woe than the actual.—*Calderon.*

May 23.

Philosophy sayeth that the body's appetites ought not to be increased by the mind. May we not reply that there is nothing in us, during this earthly prison, simply corporeal or purely spiritual? There is reason we should carry ourselves in the use of pleasure at least as favourably as we do in the pangs of grief.—*Montaigne.*

May 24.

Whatever task is of vengeance, and whatever is against forgiveness of sin, is not of the Father, but of Satan, the accuser, the father of Hell.—*William Blake.*

May 25.

When riches are gained, follow the heart; for riches are of no avail if one be weary.—*Ptah Hotep.*

May 26.

Very few men, properly speaking, live at present, but are providing to live another time.—*Swift.*

May 27.

Happiness is never our own, but always another's.—*Samaniego.*

May 28.

Life is spent in trying to strike a light in the unknown darkness.—*A. E. Waite.*

May 29.

He who knows how to shut uses no bolts—yet you cannot open. He who knows how to bind uses no cords—yet you cannot undo.—*Lao Tzu.*

May 30.

Know well thy tradesmen; for when thine affairs are in evil case, thy credit among them is a channel which may be filled.—*Ptah Hotep.*

May 31.

All corporations of men are perpetually doing injustice to individuals.... I have often reflected that though the majority of a society are honest men and would act separately with some humanity, yet, conjunctively, they are hard-hearted determined villains.—*Lord Bathurst,* 1733.

June 1.

Thou possessest the real being of all things in thy pure will, and thou art the God that thou art able to become.— *Villiers de L'Isle-Adam.*

June 2.

Dante saw Devils where I see none. I see good only. I have never known a very bad man who had not something very good about him.— *William Blake.*

June 3.

Women are by nature instructed, while the learning of men is taught them by books.— *Muir's translation of the Mahabharata.*

June 4.

Nature has good intentions but cannot carry them out. —*Aristotle.*

June 5.

The soul in this life has indeed a certain alimony, but the inadequacy of the provision compels it, in fine, to sue for the restitution of its conjugal rights.—*A. E. Waite.*

June 6.

Horace is not pleased with a slight or superficial expressing, it would betray him; he seeth more clear and further into matters; his spirit picks and ransacketh the whole storehouse of words and figures to show and present himself. The sense produceth words no longer windy or spongy, but of flesh or bone.— *Montaigne.*

June 7.

The weakest man in the world can avail himself of the passion of the wisest. The inattentive man cannot know business or do it. He who cannot command his countenance may e'en as well tell his thoughts as show them.—*Maxims of Chesterfield.*

June 8.

Peace dwelleth not in the town wherein dwell servants that are wretched.—*Ptah Hotep.*

June 9.

He who does not believe in others shall find they do not believe in him.—*Lao Tzu.*

June 10.

To face trouble is less desolating than to fear it.—*Calderon.*

June 11.

Our death conquers all our enemies.—*Spanish Romance.*

June 12.

Vice is a monster of such frightful mien
As to be hated needs but to be seen.
Yet seen too oft familiar with her face,
We first endure, then pity, then embrace.

—*Alexander Pope.*

June 13.

Woman's a creature of such beauteous mien,
That to be loved she needs but to be seen.
But once she's seen and made secure,
We first embrace, then pity, then endure.

—*Mr. Dooley.*

June 14.

Want of sympathy is the sin against the Holy Ghost.—*Anonymous.*

June 15.

The managing and employment of good wits endeareth and giveth grace unto a tongue. They bring no words unto it, but enrich their own, weigh down and cram in their signification and custom, teaching it unwonted motions.—*Montaigne.*

June 16.

For this the gods have fashioned men's grief and evil day,
That still for men hereafter might be the tale and lay.
— *William Morris.*

June 17.

Every time less than the pulsation of an artery is equal in
its tenor and value to six thousand years, for in this period
the poet's work is done, and all the great events of time start
forth and are conceived: in such a period within a moment,
a pulsation of the artery. — *William Blake.*

June 18.

If that which thou seekest thou findest not within the, I
admonish thee that thou wilt never find it without thee. —
The *Arabic of Alipi.*

June 19.

The vow of virginity is the noblest of all vows, because
it's the hardest. I wot not whether Cæsar's exploits or
Alexander's achievements exceed in hardness the resolution
of a beauteous young woman exposed to a thousand assaults
and continual pursuits yet still holding herself good and
unvanquished. There is no point of doing more thorny than
this of not doing. — *Montaigne.*

June 20.

Gérard de Nerval divined, before all the world, that
poetry should be a miracle; not a hymn to beauty nor beauty's
mirror, but beauty itself, the colour, fragrance and form of
the imagined flower, as it blossoms again out of the page.
— *Arthur Symons.*

June 21.

Be gentle and you can be bold; be frugal and you can be
liberal; avoid putting yourself before others and you can
become a leader among men. — *Lao Tzu.*

June 22.

I want nothing of the public but a healthy sense and a human heart. This does not sound much, but it is so much that the whole world would have to be turned upside down to bring it about.—*Richard Wagner.*

June 23.

A man who tells all or nothing will equally have nothing told him.—*Chesterfield.*

June 24.

It is always right to detect a fraud and perceive a folly; but it is often very wrong to expose either.—*Chesterfield.*

June 25.

Ceremony is a scarecrow to awe strike fools.—*Douglas Jerrold.*

June 26.

When a man of sense happens to be in that disagreeable situation in which he is obliged to ask himself more than once what he shall do, he will do nothing.—*Chesterfield.*

June 27.

Freedom is the one purport, wisely aimed at or unwisely, of all man's struggles, toilings and sufferings on this earth.—*Carlyle.*

June 28.

When a man reflects on his physical or moral condition he is sure to find that he is sick.—*Goethe.*

June 29.

Every failure is a step advanced
To him who will consider how it chanced.
                              —*George Meredith.*

June 30.

If your mirror be broken, look into still water; but have a care that you do not fall in.—*Hindu Proverb.*

JULY

July the First care not whether a man is Good or Bad; all I care for is whether he is a Wise man or a Fool. WILLIAM BLAKE

July 2.

Use the light that is within you to revert to your natural clearness of sight.—*Lao Tzu.*

July 3.

The sea reigns over all the mountain streams because it knows how to keep below them.—*Lao Tzu.*

July 4.

Science states, but does not explain: she is the oldest offspring of the chimeras; all the chimeras, then, on the same terms as the world (the oldest of them) are *something more* than nothing.—*Villiers de L'Isle-Adam.*

July 5.

This antique spectre malign, complex, inflexible, this illusion which science accepts for the one reality! It must be the whole effort of one's consciousness to escape from its entanglements, to dominate it, or to ignore it.—*Arthur Symons.*

July 6.

Being old we challenge most when we bring least: we are most desirous to choose when we least deserve to be accepted.—*Montaigne.*

July 7.

The pride of being, the pride of becoming—these are the two ultimate contradictions set before every idealist. That nobility of soul which comes without effort, which comes with an unrelaxed diligence in self-expression—there can at least be no comparison of its beauty with the stained and dusty onslaught on a never quite conquered enemy, in a divided self.—*Arthur Symons.*

July 8.

Where the palaces are very splendid, there the fields will be waste and the granaries empty.—*Lao Tzu.*

July 9.

The wine of life goes into vinegar, and folks that hugged the bottle shirk the cruet.—*Douglas Jerrold.*

July 10.

I do not ask of God that he should change anything in events themselves, but that he should change me in regard to things, so that I might have the power to create my own universe about me, to govern my dreams, instead of enduring them.—*Gérard de Nerval.*

July 11.

Women will readily offer rather to follow the practice of law and plead at the bar for a fee, or go to the wars for reputation, than in the midst of idleness and deliciousness be tied to keep so hard a sentinel, so dangerous a watch, as we have put upon them.—*Montaigne.*

July 12.

There is not so impudent a thing in nature as the saucy look of an assured man confident of success; the pedantic arrogance of a very husband has not so pragmatical an air. —*Congreve.*

July 13.

He who cannot hold his tongue cannot keep his friends.— *Ximenes de Enciso.*

July 14.

A man should keep his friendship in constant repair.— *Samuel Johnson.*

July 15.

You waste time to make money. You cannot heap up years as a treasure.—*Palladas of Spain.*

July 16.

Why has "to live our lives" come to mean the committing of follies?—*Anonymous.*

July 17.

Our art must be the building or an ideal world from which we may sally out, now and again, in a desperate enough attack upon the illusions in the midst of which men live.—*Arthur Symons.*

July 18.

We frame vices and weigh sins, not according to their nature, but according to our interest; whereby they take so many different unequal forms.—*Montaigne.*

July 19.

The Empire has ever been won by letting things take their course. He who must always be doing is unfit to obtain the Empire.—*Lao Tzu.*

July 20.

Action is not life, but a way of spoiling something.— *Arthur Rimbaud.*

July 21.

Life on earth is the laborious gestation of a being which is still unformed.—*A. E. Waite.*

July 22.

Joys laugh not, sorrows weep not.—*William Blake.*

July 23.

The sage is free from self-display, therefore he shines forth; from self-assertion, therefore, he is distinguished; from self-glorification, therefore, he rises superior to all. —*Lao Tzu.*

July 24.

Yet do I not repent me.—*Bunyan.*

July 25.

Words transform themselves into music, colour, shadow; a disembodied music, diaphanous colours, luminous shadow. —*Paul Verlaine.*

July 26.

False art is not expressive, but mimetic, not from experience, but from observation. True art is the flame of the last day which begins for every man when he is first moved by beauty and which seeks to burn all things until they become infinite and holy.—*W. B. Yeats.*

July 27.

Alexander said that he knew himself mortal chiefly by voluptuousness and by sleeping; sleep doth stifle and suppresseth the faculties of our soul, and voluptuousness both devoureth and dissipates them.—*Montaigne.*

July 28.

Life is a tragedy, wherein we sit as spectators awhile, and then act our part in it.—*Swift.*

July 29.

The fool denies God; the man of understanding seeks rather to deny himself.—*A. E. Waite.*

July 30.

I greedily long to make myself known, nor care I at what rate so it be truly.—*Montaigne.*

July 31.

At twenty a peacock, at thirty a lion, at forty a camel, at fifty a serpent, at sixty a dog, at seventy a monkey, and at eighty nothing. These are the ages of man.—*Gracian.*

August 1.

Do not blame the Godhead for your own creations. That is simple and eternal; you are complex and transitory. But your complexity is a varying arrangement of the very substance of that Godhead which in its simple essence appears at all times pure to itself.—*Anonymous.*

August 2.

How few successful men are interesting. The unlucky Stuarts from the first poet king . . . leave the stolid Georges millions of miles behind; sunk in their pudding and prosperity. The prosperous Elizabeth, after a life of honours, unwillingly surrendering her cosmetics up to death in a State bed; and Mary laying her head upon the block at Fotheringay after the nine-and-forty years of failure of her life (failure except of love), what unfathomable seas, and sierras upon sierras, separate them.—*Cunningham Graham.*

August 3.

Am I an old maid that I should fear the embrace of Death?—*Arthur Rimbaud.*

August 4.

Every virtue is followed by a shadow of itself which is not virtue.—*Fray Luis de Leon.*

August 5.

The sacred and profane are two in time but one in eternity.—*Anonymous.*

August 6.

I say both male and female are cast in the one same mould; instruction and custom excepted, there is no great difference between them. Plato calleth them both indifferently to the society of all studies, exercises, charges, and functions of war and peace in his Commonwealth.—*Montaigne.*

August 7.

Expect poison from standing water.—*William Blake.*

August 8.

There are few that are capable both of thought and of action. Thought expands but lames; action animates but narrows.—*Goethe.*

August 9.

Blessed is he who expects nothing; for verily he shall not be disappointed.—*Batchelor.*

August 10.

Sin is an obstruction in the heart.—*Talmud.*

August 11.

Abashed the devil stood, and felt how awful goodness is.—*Milton.*

August 12.

I have often had the fancy that there is some one myth for every man, which if we but knew it would make us understand all he did and thought.—*W. B. Yeats.*

August 13.

Speak of your sorrow and it will depart.—*Garcilaso de la Vega.*

August 14.

A man should pass part of his time with the laughters.—*Samuel Johnson.*

August 15.

There is a passion whereby mankind initiates the gods.-—*Anonymous.*

August 16.

I love measure in the feet, and number in the voice; they are gentleness that oftentimes draw no less than the face.—*Ben Jonson.*

August 17.

Some writers shun the common trodden path; but want of invention and lack of discretion looseth them. There is nothing to be seen in them hut a miserable strained affectation of strange ink-pot terms; harsh, cold, and absurd disguisements, which instead of raising pull down the matter.—*Montaigne.*

August 18.

The best commentary on the advantages of solitude is found in our experience of the average social circle.—*A. E. Waite.*

August 19.

The spiritual and the material, though we call them by different names, are, in their origin, one and the same. This sameness is a mystery—the mystery of mysteries. It is the gate of all spirituality.—*Lao Tzu.*

August 20.

A man's good breeding is his best security against other people's ill manners.—*Chesterfield.*

August 21.

The sage returns to the state of a little child.—*Lao Tzu.*

August 22.

Every space smaller than a globule of man's blood opens into eternity, of which this vegetable earth is but a shadow.—*William Blake.*

August 23.

As iron produces rust, and as wood breeds the animals that destroy it, so every state has in it the seeds of its own corruption.—*Polybius.*

August 24.

Women are not altogether in the wrong when they refuse the rules of life proscribed to the world, for as much as only men have established them without their consent.—*Montaigne.*

August 25.

Our soul does not judge as we judge; it is a capricious and hidden thing. It can be reached by a breath and be unconscious of a tempest. Let us find out what reaches it; everything is there, for it is there that we ourselves are.—*Maurice Maeterlinck.*

August 26.

The spectre (or mortal part of the mind) creates pyramids of pride and pillars in the deepest hell to reach the heavenly arches; but the immortal (part) turns his pyramids to grains of sand and his pillars to dust on the flies' wing.— *William Blake.*

August 27.

I bequeath my sword to him that shall succeed me in my pilgrimage, and my courage and skill to him that can get it. — *Bunyan.*

August 28.

I nor acknowledge nor discern in Aristotle the most part of my ordinary motions. They are clothed with other robes, and shrouded for the use of academical schools. God send them well to speed; but were I of the trade I would naturalise art as much as they artise nature. When I write I can well omit the company and spare the remembrance of books.— *Montaigne.*

August 29.

The treasures of heaven are not negations of passion, but realities of intellect from which the passions emanate uncurbed in their eternal glory.— *William Blake.*

August 30.

A good man out of the good treasure of the heart bringeth forth good things; and an evil man out of the evil treasure bringeth forth evil things.—St. Matt. xii. 35.

August 31.

When merit has been achieved do not take it to yourself; for if you do not take it to yourself, it shall never be taken from you.— *Lao Tzu .*

September 1.

Every man is the child of his own works.— *Cervantes.*

September 2.

It is not the battle of life that weighs down the soul, but its grey skies, its monotony.—*A. E. Waite.*

September 3.

Painting, poetry, and music are the three powers in man of conversing with Paradise, not swept away by the flood of time and space.—*William Blake.*

September 4.

Isocrates said that the town of Athens pleased men even as ladies do whom we serve for affection. Everyone loved to come thither, to walk and pass away the time, but none affected to wed it; that is to say to endenison, to dwell and habituate himself therein.—*Montaigne.*

September 5.

Hood an ass with revered purple, so you can hide his too ambitious ears, and he shall pass for a cathedral doctor.—*Ben Jonson.*

September 6.

Words are living things, which we have not created; they go their way without asking our leave to live. Words are suspicious, not without malice; they resist mere force with the impalpable resistance of fire or water.—*Paul Verlaine.*

September 7.

If a man would enter into Noah's rainbow and make a friend of one of the images of wonder which dwell there entreating him to leave mortal things; then would he arise from the grave and meet the Lord in the air.—*William Blake.*

September 8.

In the highest antiquity the people did not know that they had rulers. In the next age they loved and praised them. In the next they feared them. In the next they despised them.—*Lao Tzu.*

September 9.

If a man were to ask of nature the reason of her creative activity, and if she were willing to give ear and answer, she would say, "Ask me not, but understand in silence: even as I am silent and am not wont to speak."—*Plotinus.*

September 10.

If the spirit of God's love is as a breath over the world, suggesting, strengthening the love which it desires, seeking man that man may seek God, itself the impulse which it humbles itself to accept at man's hands; how much more is this love of God, in its inconceivable acceptance and exchange, the most divine, the only unending intoxication in the world.—*Arthur Symons.*

September 11.

The more steps and degrees there are, the more delight and honour is there on the top.—*Montaigne.*

September 12.

It is easy to conceal the nakedness of the body: it is not easy to hide that of the mind.—*A. E. Waite.*

September 13.

Think more of missing once, than of hitting the mark a hundred times.—*Gracian.*

September 14.

Poverty many can endure with dignity. Success how few can carry off even with decency and without bearing their innermost infirmities before the public gaze.—*Cunningham Graham.*

September 15.

Baudelaire, in whom the spirit is always an uneasy guest at the orgie of life, had a certain theory of Realism which tortures many of his poems into strange metallic shapes, and fills them with initiative odours and disturbs them with a too deliberate rhetoric of the flesh.—*Arthur Symons.*

September 16.

Let us confess there are few among us that had not rather be a thief and a church robber and have his wife a murderer and a heretic, than not have her more chaste than himself.—*Montaigne.*

September 17.

The soul of sweet delight can never be defiled.—*William Blake.*

September 18.

In a symbol there is concealment and yet revelation: hence therefore by silence and by speech acting together comes a double significance.—*T. Carlyle.*

September 19.

The cautious man flourisheth, the exact one is praised; the innermost chamber openeth unto the man of silence. Wide is the seat of the man gentle of speech; but knives are prepared against one that forceth a path.—*Kegemni.*

September 20.

She likes herself, yet others hates
For that which in herself she prizes,
And while she laughs at them forgets
She is the thing that she despises.
—*Congreve.*

September 21.

Solemnity serves many for capacity.—*Yriarte.*

September 22.

It is only when we have returned to the dust that we shall understand our kinship with the stars.—*Anonymous.*

September 23.

All love is an attempt to break through the loneliness of individuality, to give and to receive that element which remains so cold and so invincible in the midst of the soul. —*Arthur Symons.*

September 24.

Nothing is so detestable as the majority.—Goethe.

September 25.

Thou fearest not to offend nature's universal and undoubted laws, and art moved at thine own partial and fantastical ones.—*Montaigne.*

September 26.

The best soldiers are not warlike; the best fighters do not lose their temper. The greatest conquerors are those who overcome their enemies without strife.— *Lao Tzu.*

September 27.

We feed full well and drink like beasts, but they are not actions that hinder the offices of our mind; whereas voluptuousness brings each other thought under subjection, and by its imperious authority makes brutish and dullish all Plato's philosophy and divinity; and yet he complains not of it.—*Montaigne.*

September 28.

Half the world spends its time laughing at the follies of the other half; and all are fools.—*Gracian.*

September 29.

There are beings who can spread wings that grow in an instant, stand on feet that pass like the pattering of a rain shower. They can make a little flower live; they can make all things that we can only destroy. They can give the life we have learned to waste. Yet they do not boast—they leave that to us.—*Anonymous.*

September 30.

There is something almost vulgar in happiness which does not become joy, and joy is an ecstasy which can rarely be maintained in the soul for more than the moment during which we recognise that it is not sorrow.—*Arthur Symons.*

OCTOBER

October the First
Rose would
have been Proud
if it had not been born
among Thorns
RAYMON LULL

October 2.

It is shameful to confuse a mean mind. If thou be about to do what is in thine heart, overcome it as a thing rejected of princes. Neither question the poor man to please thine heart, nor pour out thy wrath upon him.—*Ptah Hotep.*

October 3.

If that which bears all things bears thee, bear thou and be borne.—*Palladas.*

October 4.

Sensuality is never more than the malady of love.—*Arthur Symons.*

October 5.

It astonishes me more than anything else to see the rest of the world unastonished at its helplessness.—*Pascal.*

October 6.

It is the foulness of the peacock's feet which doth abate his pride, and stoop his gloating-eyed tail.— *Montaigne.*

October 7.

But who is it that knows the real cause of Heaven's hatred? This is why the sage finds it difficult to act.—*Lao Tzu.*

October 8.

Blood comes by birth, vice by contagion.—*Aleman.*

October 9.

Whoever is right, the persecutor must be wrong.— *William Penn.*

October 10.

When the soul gives itself absolutely to love all the barriers of the world are burnt away; they no longer exist anymore than they exist for children or for God.—*Arthur Symons.*

October 11.

Man does not perceive the truth, but God perceives the truth in man. The inner light is the natural ascent of the spirit within us which at last illuminates and transfigures those who tend it.—*Jacob Boehme.*

October 12.

I hate a wayward and sad disposition, that glideth over the pleasures of his life, and fattens and feeds on miseries.—*Montaigne.*

October 13.

Life is logic gone astray.—*Henri Bergson.*

October 14.

In the Life process the disproportion between desire and accomplishment is absurd. Sometimes desire dies out; sometimes opposition kills it; sometimes it is distracted from what it would do by what it has done. Enchanted by its own face in a mirror. Like dust raised by the wind we living creatures turn on ourselves while the wind goes on.—*Henri Bergson.*

October 15.

As we realise the identity of a poem, a prayer, or a kiss, in that spiritual universe which we are weaving for ourselves; as we realise the infinite insignificance of action, its immense difference from the current of our real life, it is with relief we turn to the doctrine of Plotinus, so much more likely to be true because it has so much the air of a dream.—*Arthur Symons.*

October 16.

For in the particular acts of human life it is not the interior soul and the true man, but the spectral shade of the man alone which laments and weeps, performing his part on earth as in an ample and extended scene in which many spectral souls and phantom scenes appear.—*Plotinus.*

October 17.

It is against the nature of love not to be violent and against the condition of violence to be constant.— *Montaigne.*

October 18.

Great God! I'd rather be
A Pagan suckled in a creed outworn,
So I might, standing on this pleasant lea,
Have glimpses that would make me less forlorn,
Have sight of Proteus rising from the sea,
As hear old Triton blow his wreathed horn.
— *Wordsworth.*

October 19.

You cannot spend one vacant hour alone. You run, a self-deserter, and allay your cares now with wine and now with sleep.—*Horace.*

October 20.

Some people must live alone even in the midst of cities, in the midst of embraces.—*Anonymous.*

October 21.

It is a great relief to sinners to find themselves sinned against.—*Anonymous.*

October 22.

Words are of value only as a notation of the free breath of the spirit; they must be chosen and set carefully to reflect and chime upon one another, not for their own sake, but for what they can never, except by suggestion, express. The word is the philtre of the evocation; chosen as a liberating principle by which spirit is extracted from matter and perhaps assumes an immortal nature.— *Le Maître Stephané Mallarme.*

October 23.

The greatest man accepts the greatest risks.— *Henri Bergson.*

October 24.

Let us teach ladies to know how to prevail, highly to esteem themselves, to amuse, to circumvent, and cozen us. —*Montaigne.*

October 25.

A man has generally the good or ill qualities he attributes to mankind.—*Shenstone.*

October 26.

Shakespeare wrote at a time when solitary great men were gathering to themselves the fire that had once flowed hither and thither among all men, when individualism in work and thought and emotion was breaking up: the old rhythms of life, no longer uplifted by the myths of Christianity and of still older faiths, were sinking into the earth.—*W. B. Yeats.*

October 27.

To be perfectly secret one must be so by nature, not by obligation.—*Montaigne.*

October 28.

Monstrous discords and escapades of orchestration fling us from emotion to emotion. No animal orgie can effect that dissipation of being which is wrought by those avalanches of sound, those tremblings of suggested melody, or the reiteration which melts the heart like wax and blinds the eyes with mists of passion.—*Anonymous.*

October 29.

I most commonly travel without company, which is a great help for continued reasonings: whereby I have sufficient leisure to entertain myself.—*Montaigne.*

October 30.

Let us be as strange as if we had been married a great while and as well bred as if we were not married at all.—*Congreve.*

October 31.

The Dictionary is the only book worth a poet's reading.—*Théophile Gautier.*

November 1.

The matrimonial nest is natural, but it would be more tolerable if it were tempered by migration.—*Anonymous.*

November 2.

Many people do not know how to read—unless it is the newspapers.—*Le Maître Stephané Mallarme.*

November 3.

He who has not learned that honour is tarnished by a breath is more fortunate than he is honourable.—*Calderon.*

November 4.

I have heard indeed of some virtuous persons but never of any virtuous nation.—*Dryden.*

November 5.

There is a method in a man's wickedness. It grows up by degrees.—*Beaumont and Fletcher.*

November 6.

Public Institutions are only trees for the public conscience to go to roost upon.—*Godolphin.*

November 7.

Human longings are perversely obstinate; and to the man whose mouth is watering for a peach, it is no use to offer the largest vegetable marrow.—*George Eliot.*

November 8.

How can one write songs of hatred without hating? And how could I, to whom culture and barbarism are alone of importance, hate the French nation, which is among the most cultivated of the earth, and to whom I owe, a great part of my own cultivation?—*Goethe.*

November 9.

Once love finds itself bounded only by its own capacity its ecstasy is flawless; so far does the love of God exceed the love of the creature; and so far would it exceed that love if God did not exist.—*Arthur Symons.*

November 10.

Do I not lively display myself? That sufficeth. I have what I will. All the world may know me by my book, and my book by me.—*Montaigne.*

November 11.

Do I not look into a woman's eyes,
And all I feel throngs to her heart and brain.
Clouded in eternal mystery seen or unseen I am near her.
Let her call it what she will—Joy, Love, Heart, God—
I have no name. Feeling is everything. A name is Sound
    and smoke clouding Heaven's glow.

> —*Goethe.*

November 12.

We contract marriages as we contract fevers, partly through pure misfortune, but largely through negligence.— *A. E. Waite.*

November 13.

Love is a passion that commixeth with small store of solid essence, great quantity of doting vanity, and fabriciant raving: it must therefore be requited and served with the like.—*Montaigne.*

November 14.

Love is a desire of the infinite in humanity, and as humanity has its limits it can but return sadly upon itself when that limit is reached. So human love is not only an ecstasy, but a despair, and the more profound a despair the more ardently it is returned.—*Arthur Symons.*

November 15.

There have been men who loved the future like a mistress, and the future mixed her breath into their breath and shook her hair about them and hid them from the understanding of their times.—*W. B. Yeats.*

November 16.

We all like to take and run. The natural man is a thief.—*Anonymous.*

November 17.

Carlyle complains that there is nothing of Falstaff in Christ. But he, who cursed the fig-tree because it bore no fruit when he desired fruit, had many other points of sympathy with the champion of immortal Debauch.—*Anonymous.*

November 18.

Life is a perpetual changing of something that wishes to stand still.—*Henri Bergson.*

November 19.

Stephani Mallarmé was one of those who love literature too much to write it except by fragments; in whom the desire of perfection brings its own defeat.—*Arthur Symons.*

November 20.

In dreaming, the next morning I can well call to mind what colour my dreams were of, whether blithe, sad, or strange, but what in substance, the more I labour to find out the more I overwhelm them in oblivion. So of casual and unpremeditated conceits that come into my brain, nought but a vain image of them remaineth in my memory, so much only as sufficeth unprofitably to make me chafe, spite and fret in pursuit of them.—*Montaigne.*

November 21.

The greater the number of laws and enactments the more thieves and robbers there will be.—*Lao Tzu.*

November 22.

Give us beer and a kitchen-wench that we may live in soberness and sense.—*Anonymous.*

November 23.

Alas! poor, silly man, thou hast but too, too many necessary and avoidable incommodities without increaseing them by thine own invention, thou aboundest in real and essential deformities, and need not forge any by imagination.—*Montaigne.*

November 24.

The true aim of education is to develop a real love of beauty.—*Plato.*

November 25.

A symbol is a transparent lamp about a spiritual flame.—*W. B. Yeats.*

November 26.

He who does not rise with the sun does not enjoy the day.—*Cervantes.*

November 27.

The material body does not represent an assembly of "means employed," but an assembly of obstacles overcome: it represents a limitation of active purpose.—*Henri Bergson.*

November 28.

The merit of originality is not novelty, it is sincerity.—*Carlyle.*

November 29.

Nothing reveals character so much as what a man thinks laughable. A clever man thinks almost everything laughable: a wise man almost nothing.—*Goethe.*

November 30.

It is not so much that men must work and women must weep, but that men may laugh and women must look shocked.—*Anonymous.*

December 1.

I believe that the borders of our memories are a part of one great memory, the memory of nature herself.— *W. B. Yeats.*

December 2.

The old beauty is no longer beautiful and the new truth is no longer true.— *Julian the Apostate.*

December 3.

Become the flower of thyself! Thou art but what thou thinkest: therefore think thyself eternal. If thou cease to limit in thyself a thing, that is, to desire it, if, in so doing, thou withdraw thyself from it, it will follow thee, woman-like, as the water fills the place that is offered to it in the hollow of the hand.— *Villiers de L' Isle-Adam.*

December 4.

Blake held that the men who ate from the tree of knowledge wasted their days in anger against one another, and in taking one another captive in great nets. Men who sought their food among the green leaves of the Tree of Life condemned none but the unimaginative and the idle, and those that forgot that even love .and death and old age are an imaginative art.— *W. B. Yeats.*

December 5.

An aching body and a mind
Not wholly clear or wholly blind,
Too keen to test, too weak to find,
Are God's worst portion to mankind.
              — *Matthew Arnold.*

December 6.

The poet that fails in writing becomes often a morose critic. The weak and insipid white-wine makes at length a figure in vinegar.— *Shenstone.*

December 7.

All Balzac's characters are gifted with Balzac's ardour of life; his fictions are deeply coloured as dreams. Each mind is a weapon loaded to the muzzle with will. The very scullions have genius.—*Baudelaire.*

December 8.

It is in working within limits that the master reveals himself.—*Goethe.*

December 9.

Emerson wrote over the door of his library the word "Whim."

December 10.

The lacerating laughter of the idealist is never surer in its aim than when it turns the arms of science against itself. Wit sharpened to a fineness of irony such as only wit which is also philosophy can attain. Satire which becomes tragic, fantastic, macabre in its persecution of the ugly.—*Anonymous.*

December 11.

Stupidity is more criminal than vice: if only because vice is curable, stupidity incurable.—*Arthur Symons.*

December 12.

The philosopher Antisthenes took away all distinction between women's virtue and ours. It is much more easy to accuse the one sex than to excuse the other.—*Montaigne.*

December 13.

I held life fast and stared into her eyes. They are blank and cruel. She screamed and raged when I forced her to tell me her name. But at last she ceased to struggle and put her arms round my neck, saying: "My name is Death."—*Anonymous.*

December 14.

To die! Evidently, one dies without knowing it, as every night one passes into sleep. Evidently. But to be no more, to be here no more, to be ours no more! Not even to be able, any more, one idle afternoon, to press against one's human heart, the ancient sadness contained in one little chord on the piano!—*Jules Laforgue.*

December 15.

He that speaks all he knows doth cloy and distaste us. Who feareth to express himself, leadeth our conceit to imagine more than haply he conceiveth.—*Montaigne.*

December 16.

Walls may have ears as long as they have not tongues.—*Levis de Ulloa.*

December 17.

She who escapeth safe and unpolluted from out the school of freedom giveth more confidence of herself than she who cometh sound out of the school of severity and restraint.—*Montaigne.*

December 18.

The roadway of excess leads to the palace of wisdom.—*William Blake.*

December 19.

Read the features of thy foe, wherever he may find thee;
Small he is, seen face to face, but thrice his size behind thee.

—*George Meredith.*

December 20.

It was with precise accuracy that Whistler applied the terms of music to his painting, for painting, when it aims at being the vision of reality; not colour, nothing but gradation of colour, passes almost into the condition of music.—*Arthur Symons.*

December 21.

Women are rare and difficult virtues; so soon as they are ours we are no longer theirs.—*Montaigne.*

December 22.

Day by day we are born as night retires; possessing nothing of our former life, strangers to yesterday.—*Palladas.*

December 23.

The Illuminati know how to penetrate into the knowledge of that clear ether wherein the subtlest sensation is transfused into an orchestra of light beyond all wonder.—*Anonymous.*

December 24.

In cogitation the thought or attention flits aimlessly about the subject.

In meditation it circles round it; it views it systematically, from all sides, gaining perspective.

In contemplation it radiates from a centre, that is, as light from the sun it reaches out in an infinite number of ways to things that are related to or dependent on it.

—*Richard of St. Victor.*

December 25.

He the divine child is here a-wearied
Of weeping the earth pain. Here for his rest would he
Cease from his mourning, only a little while.
Sith sleepeth this child here, still ye the branches.

—*Ezra Pound, from Lope di Vega.*

December 26.

We hear tales of the celebrated swimmer who dived a distance of eighty stadia to give the Greeks warning of the Persian advance. If, however, I may offer an opinion on the subject, I should say that he came in a boat.—*Herodotus.*

December 27.

Alas! what sorrow and tears our fathers cost us.—*The Cid.*

December 28.

Charity for mankind, dignity for oneself, and sincerity for God.—*George Sand.*

December 29.

The shortest path to fame is that which winds.—*Gracian.*

December 30.

You never know the ecstasy of heaven until you have mixed it in the bowl of earth.—*Anonymous.*

December 31.

If the fool would persist in his folly he would become wise.—*William Blake.*

BIBLIOGRAPHY

Farr, Florence. *The Dancing Faun.* London: Elkin Mathews and John Lane, 1894.

Farr, Florence. *Egyptian Magic.* Collectanea Hermetica Vol. VIII. London: Theosophical Publishing Society, 1896.
___. Expanded with "Preface to the Collectanea Hermetica Series" by R.A. Gilbert, and "Introduction" by Timothy D'Arch Smith. "Studies in Hermetic Tradition." Wellingborough: Aquarian Press, 1982.

Farr, Florence. *The Enochian Experiments of the Golden Dawn: the Enochian Alphabet Clairvoyantly Examined.* Edited with Introductory Note by Darcy Küntz. Holmes Publishing Group, 1996.

Farr, Florence. *The Magic of a Symbol.* Introductory Note by Darcy Küntz. Holmes Publishing Group, 1996.

Farr, Florence. *Modern Woman: Her Intentions.* London: Frank Palmer, 1910.

Farr, Florence. *The Music of Speech, Containing the Words of Some Poets, Thinkers and Music-makers Regarding the Practice of the Bardic Art, Together with Fragments of Verse Set to Its Own Melody.* London: Elkin Mathews, MDCCCCIX. [1909].

Farr, Florence. *The Mystery of Time. A Masque.* London: Theosophical Publishing Society, 1905.

Farr, Florence. *The Serpent's Path: The Magical Plays of Florence Farr*. Introductory Note by Darcy Küntz. Holmes Publishing Group, 2001.

Farr, Florence. *The Solemnization of Jacklin: Some Adventures on the Search for Reality*. London: A.C. Fifeld. 1912.

Farr, Florence (as F. Farr Emery). *The Way of Wisdom. An Investigation of the Meanings of the Letters of the Hebrew Alphabet, Considered as a Remnant of Chaldean Wisdom*. London: J. M. Watkins, 1900.

Periodicals

The Lamp. Conducted by Albert E.S. Smith.
Toronto, Canada: Privately printed.

"The Tree of Life," Vol. IV: No. 7 (No. 43), 15 September 1900. pp. 194-197.

The Occult Review. Edited by Ralph Shirley.
London: William Rider & Son Ltd.

"The Magic of a Symbol". Vol. VII, No. 2, February 1908. pp. 82-93.
"Egyptian Use of Symbols". Vol. VII, No. 3, March 1908. pp. 146-149.
"On the Kabalah". Vol. VII, No. 4, April 1908. pp. 213-218.
"The Rosicrucians and Alchemists". Vol. VII, No. 5, May 1908. pp. 259-264.
"The Philosophy Called Vedanta". Vol. VII: No. 6, June 1908. pp. 333-338.
"The Tetrad, or Structure of the Mind". Vol. VIII: No. 1, July 1908. pp. 34-40.
"On the Play of the Image-Maker". Vol. VIII: No. 2, August 1908. pp. 87-91.

The Theosophical Review.
Edited by Annie Besant and G.R.S. Mead.
London: Theosophical Publishing Society.

"The Mystery of Time: A Masque". Vol. 36: No. 211, March 1905, pp. 9-19.
"A Dialogue of Vision". Vol. 39: No. 229, May 1906. pp. 77-84.

Contributions

A Lover of Philalethes. *A Short Enquiry Concerning the Hermetic Art.* Collectanea Hermetica Vol. III. Edited by W. Wynn Westcott. "An Introduction to Alchemy" by Florence Farr (as S.S.D.D.). London: Theosophical Publishing Society, [1894].

Vaughan, Thomas (as Eugenius Philalethes). *Euphrates; or, The Waters of the East.* Commentary by Florence Farr (as S.S.D.D.). Collectanea Hermetica Vol. VII. London: Theosophical Publishing Society, 1896.

Westcott, W. Wynn. *The Golden Dawn Court Cards as Drawn by William Wynn Westcott.* Introduction by Anthony Fleming. Contains "R.R. et A.C. Colour Scheme" from the note-book of S.S.D.D. Holmes Publishing Group, 1996.

Biographies

Edgar, David. "Ticket to Milford Haven." *London Review of Books.* (21 September 2006): pp. 11-12.

Cogdill, Sharon E. "Florence Farr's Sphere Group: The Secret Society within the Golden Dawn." in *Cauda Pavonis*, Vol. XI, No. 1, (Spring, 1992), pp. 7-12.

Greer, Mary K. *Women of the Golden Dawn: Rebels and Priestesses.* Rochester, VT: Park Street Press, 1995.

Harper, George Mills. *Yeats's Golden Dawn*. London: Macmillan, 1974.

Hough, Graham Goulden. *The Mystery Religion of W.B. Yeats*. Harvester Press, 1984.

Johnson, Josephine. *Florence Farr: Bernard Shaw's New Woman*. Gerrards Cross: Colin Smythe, 1975.

King, Francis. *Ritual Magic in England*. [n.p.:] Neville Spearman, 1970.

Laity, Cassandra. "W.B. Yeats and Florence Farr: The Influence of the 'New Woman' Actress on Yeats's Changing Images of Women." *Modern Drama*. 4 (1985), pp. 620-637.

Litz, A. Walton "Florence Farr: A 'Transitional' Woman." Maria DiBattista ed., and Lucy McDiarmid ed. *High and Low Moderns: Literature and Culture, 1889-1939*. New York; Oxford: Oxford University Press, 1996. pp. 85-106.

Mack, Maynard ed., Leonard Fellows Dean ed., and William Frost ed. *Modern Poetry*. (1950). Englewood Cliffs, NJ: Prentice-Hall, 1961.

Peters, Margot. *Bernard Shaw and the Actresses*. Doubleday and Co., 1980.

Tully, Caroline. "Florence and the Mummy" in *Women's Voices in Magic*. Edited by Brandy Williams. Megalithica Books, 2009, pp. 15-23.

NOTES

ON THE

"CONTRIBUTORS."

DARCY KÜNTZ is the director of the Golden Dawn Research Trust which was founded in 1998. The Research Trust is preserving the teachings, ritual, history, practices, documents, letters, and books of the Hermetic Order of the Golden Dawn (as it existed between the dates 1887-1930). We are preserving this material so that the information may be available and remain accessible to scholars now and in the future. Some of his published work includes: *Complete Golden Dawn Cipher Manuscript* (1996); *Golden Dawn Sourcebook* (1996); *The Historic Structure of the Original Golden Dawn Temples* (1999); *The Golden Dawn American Source Book* (2000); *Sent From the Second Order* (2005); *Ancient Texts of the Golden Rosicrucians* (2008).

CAROLINE WISE is a former owner of Atlantis Bookshop in London. In 1989 she instigated the re-publication of the works of Kennneth Grant while at Skoob Books. In 1993 she produced the Egyptian magic themed plays that Florence Farr co-wrote with Olivia Shakespear, and has written and presented ritual readings of them several times since. She has a particular interest in bringing the women in the Golden Dawn and other women mystics and magicians of the past to to a wider audience. Caroline is an Arch Priestess in the Fellowship of Isis and gives presentations in the UK, USA and Europe on the Goddess.

I have received.

Yours faithfully

Florence Emery.